SEWING IN NO TIME

SEWING IN NO TIME

50 STEP-BY-STEP WEEKEND PROJECTS MADE EASY

EMMA HARDY

CICO BOOKS
LONDON NEW YORK

NOTE:
Unless otherwise stated, all fabric quantities
given in the projects are based on fabric that
is 135 cm/54 in. wide.

First published in 2008 by CICO Books
an imprint of Ryland Peters & Small
20–21 Jockey's Fields, London WC1R 4BW

10 9 8 7 6 5 4 3 2 1

Text © Emma Hardy 2008
Design and photography © CICO Books 2008

A CIP catalogue record for this book is available from
the British Library

ISBN-13: 978 1 906094 25 6
ISBN-10: 1 906094 25 X

Printed in China

Editor: Sarah Hoggett
Designer: David Fordham
Illustrator: Michael Hill
Photographer: Debbie Patterson
Stylist: Emma Hardy

Contents

Introduction

I've enjoyed sewing ever since I was a child. My mother taught me the basic stitches, which I used to make doll's clothes, blankets and costumes by hand, progressing to making my own clothes as I got older and had mastered the sewing machine. I loved being able to create designs that were unique, individual and allowed me to express myself.

I still very much delight in this process – but these days, the demands of modern life mean that I am short of time. With this in mind, I have put together 50 projects that are quick and easy to make. From bed linen and cushions to window treatments, storage ideas and table linen, the projects are both practical and decorative and most can be made in a matter of hours. A basic sewing kit and sewing machine are all that you need, and most of the projects are ideal for a novice – although I hope that the designs will appeal to the experienced stitcher as well as the beginner.

Each beautifully photographed design is accompanied by charmingly illustrated instructions that lead you step by step through the projects. Each project also includes an estimated timing, although this is only a guide: the actual time will vary depending on your experience and expertise. The techniques section at the back of the book gives a simple guide to basic skills and the book also contains all the templates that you need to complete the projects.

Choose fabrics that will complement and coordinate with your décor and home furnishings, or tailor-make projects to create special gifts for friends and family. Experiment with colours, patterns and trimmings, collecting ribbons, braids and vintage buttons to give your creations the perfect finishing touches. With such a wide selection of wonderful fabrics currently on sale from craft and sewing shops and online companies, I hope you will be inspired to use this book as a starting point to create your own designs.

CHAPTER 1

Relaxation spaces

Floral cushion cover with ties

Add a pretty, country feel to your sofa with these lovely floral cushions. I used the same fabric throughout, but you could choose a coordinating fabric for the back, so that you can turn the cushion over and change the look to suit your mood.

The covers are very easy to make, as they have no zips or buttons but are fastened with neat little fabric ties. To make them even simpler, you could replace the ties with ribbon.

YOU WILL NEED

75 cm/30 in. floral fabric
Sewing machine and matching sewing thread
45-cm/18-in. square cushion pad

Take 1.5-cm/½-in. seam allowances throughout unless otherwise stated.

1. Cut a piece of fabric measuring 48 x 49 cm/19 x 19¼ in. Along one short edge, fold over 1 cm/⅜ in. and then another 1.5 cm/½ in. to the wrong side. Machine stitch in place.

2. Cut four 7 x 25-cm/3 x 10-in. strips of fabric. Fold each one in half, wrong sides together, and press. Open out. Along both long sides, fold over 1.5 cm/½ in. to the wrong side and press. At one short end, fold over 1.5 cm/½ in. and press.

3. Fold the whole strip in half along the centre fold line. Machine stitch along the strip, stitching as close to the unfolded edge as possible, and across the folded end. Press.

4. Cut a 48 x 19-cm/19 x 7½-in. rectangle of fabric. Along one long edge, fold over 1 cm/³⁄₈ in. and then another 1.5 cm/½ in. to the wrong side. Pin and machine stitch.

5. Cut a 48-cm/19-in. square of fabric. With right sides together, pin the raw edge of the rectangle from Step 4 to one side of the square, inserting one tie into the seam 12 cm/4½ in. from one corner and another one 12 cm/4½ in. from the other corner. Machine stitch in place. Press the seam open.

6. Lay this piece wrong side down on your work surface. With right sides together, place the other piece of fabric from Step 1 on top, aligning the hemmed side with the seam on the bottom piece.

7. Fold the flap over the top and pin and machine stitch around the three sides of the square. Turn the cover right side out.

8. Take the remaining two ties, fold under 1.5 cm/½ in. at the raw ends and machine stitch them onto the cushion cover, aligning them with the ties alredy in place. Press the cover. Insert the cushion pad and tie the ties in a neat bow to close.

Compass, pencil and paper
for pattern

25 cm/10 in. each of a selection
of patterned fabrics

50 cm/20 in. natural-coloured
linen

45-cm/18-in. square cushion pad

35-cm/14-in. zip

Sewing machine and matching
sewing thread

Dotty patchwork cushion | 2 hours |

Stitch large circles of patterned fabric onto plain linen to make this delightfully dotty cushion cover. Choose scraps of your favourite fabrics for the dots and edge them with a small zigzag stitch to prevent them from fraying.

1. Using a compass, draw a circle 13 cm/5 in. in diameter on paper. Cut out and use as a paper pattern. Pin to the fabrics and cut out nine fabric circles.

2. Cut two 48-cm/19-in. squares of linen. Lay one piece right side up on your work surface and arrange the fabric circles on top, leaving 1 cm/³⁄₈ in. between each one and 3.5 cm/1½ in. all the way around the edge. Using a small zigzag stitch on the sewing machine, stitch all around the fabric circles staying as close to the edge as you can.

3. With right sides together, tack the two linen squares together along one side using the seam allowance. Machine stitch from each corner for 5 cm/2 in. Press the seam open and lay the zip right side down on the wrong side of the seam. Tack and then machine stitch the zip in place. Remove the tacking stitches.

4. With right sides together, pin and machine stitch the remaining three sides of the fabric squares together. Snip the corners, open the zip and turn the cushion cover right side out. Press. Insert the cushion pad.

Scatter cushion with ribbon stripes

2 hours

This is the perfect way to use up all those leftover bits of ribbon that never seem to be quite long enough to be useful. Collect together ribbons and braids in similar colours and stitch them onto plain fabric to make a stylish cushion cover that no one would guess was made from scraps.

YOU WILL NEED

50 cm/20 in. plain fabric
Selection of ribbons in toning colours and various widths
Sewing machine
Matching sewing thread
35 x 50-cm/13¾ x 20-in. cushion pad
3 buttons

Take 1.5-cm/½-in. seam allowances throughout unless otherwise stated.

1. Cut two 40 x 39-cm/15¾ x 15¼-in. rectangles of plain fabric. Fold over and press 1 cm/⅜ in. to the wrong side along one 40-cm/15¾-in. edge of each piece. Fold over another 1.5 cm/½ in. on one piece and 5 cm/2 in. on the other and machine stitch close to the edge.

2. Make three buttonholes along this wider border (see page 164) to fit the size of the buttons you are using.

3. Cut a 38 x 53-cm/15 x 21-in. rectangle of plain fabric. Lay it on your work surface and place the ribbons on it until you are happy with the arrangement. Pin them in place, then tack and machine stitch each one onto the fabric.

4. Lay the ribbon-covered piece right side up on your work surface, with the buttonholed back piece right side down on top, aligning the raw edges. Place the other back piece right side down on top, again aligning the raw edges, and pin in place. Machine stitch around the edges, trim the corners to reduce bulk and turn right side out. Sew three buttons onto the back in the required position. Press. Insert the cushion pad.

Yo-yo cushion

YOU WILL NEED

25-cm/10-in. lengths of a selection of small-patterned fabrics

Paper for template

Pencil and compass

Needle and thread

Shop-bought cushion cover to fit 35-cm/14-in. square pad

35-cm/14-in. square cushion pad

This is the perfect introduction to simple sewing. The yo-yos are made from scraps of patterned fabric, stitched onto a shop-bought cover to create an inexpensive but very decorative cushion. If you're making a cushion in a different size, remember that the finished yo-yos will be about half the size of the original circle. It's also best to make all the yo-yos from the same weight of fabric; lightweight dress cotton is ideal.

> **Rosettes: 5 minutes each** **Whole project: 4 hours**

1. Using a compass, draw a circle 12 cm/4¾ in. in diameter on paper. Cut out and pin the template onto your fabric. Cut out 36 circles from a variety of fabrics. Turn over about 5 mm/¼ in. to the wrong side and press all the way around.

2. Work a line of running stitches around each circle close to the fold. Pull the thread to gather and secure with a few stitches.

3. Arrange the rosettes on your work surface in six rows of six, making sure that no two rosettes of the same fabric are next to one another. Stitch each row together with a few small stitches, and then stitch the six rows together in the same way to form a panel.

4. Lay the panel on the front of the cushion cover and hand stitch it in place by working a few stitches at the widest point of each rosette and a few stitches around the inner edges to hold everything securely in place.

Floral floor rug

For a quick-and-easy way to bring pattern into a room without completely redecorating, why not make this pretty fireside rug? Made from vintage-style, floral fabric edged with a ruffled border that picks up one of the colours in the main fabric, it is as decorative as it is useful. A wide velvet ribbon in a contrast colour provides a lovely finishing touch. Choose a heavyweight furnishing fabric that will withstand a bit of wear and tear.

YOU WILL NEED

50 cm/20 in. plain fabric for the frill
1 m/40 in. heavyweight floral cotton or furnishing fabric
1.5 m/60 in. velvet ribbon
Sewing machine
Needle and matching sewing thread

Take 1.5-cm/¹⁄₂-in. seam allowances throughout unless otherwise stated.

1. Cut two 15 x 150-cm/6 x 59-in. strips of plain fabric for the frill. With right sides together, fold in half lengthways and machine stitch along both short ends. Turn right side out and press. Work a line of running stitches about 1 cm/³⁄₈ in. from the raw edge along the whole length. Pull the thread to gather the fabric so that the frill is 54 cm/21¹⁄₄ in. long. Secure with a few stitches at the end.

2. Cut two 57 x 75-cm/22¹⁄₂ x 29¹⁄₂-in. rectangles of floral fabric and two 60-cm/23¹⁄₂-in. lengths of velvet ribbon. Pin and machine stitch one ribbon onto each short end of one of the floral pieces 5 cm/2 in. from the edge.

3. With right sides together, aligning the raw edges, lay one frill along each short end of the floral fabric to which you stitched the ribbon. Pin and tack in place.

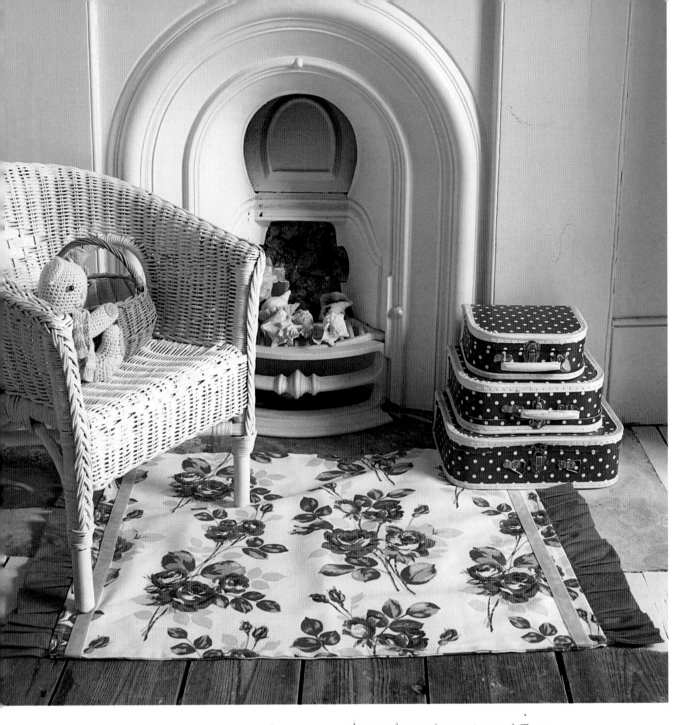

4. With right sides together, lay the other floral piece on top. Pin and machine stitch all the way around, leaving a 20-cm/8-in. opening along one long side. Trim the corners, turn right side out and press. Hand stitch the opening closed. Top stitch all the way around the rug 1 cm/³⁄₈ in. from the edge.

Lampshade with ruffled trim

This is the perfect way to transform a plain, shop-bought lampshade; the same technqiue can be used on shades of any shape or size. Just gather up ribbon with a simple running stitch and finish with a thin ribbon or braid around the middle.

1 hour

1. Work a line of running stitch along the centre of the wide ribbon and pull the thread to gather the ribbon. Check that the gathered ribbon fits neatly around the base of your lampshade, then finish with a few small stitches at the end to hold the ruffles in place.

YOU WILL NEED

Small square lampshade

Enough 22-mm-/1½-in.-wide ribbon to go roughly six times around the base of your lampshade

Needle and thread

Sewing machine and matching sewing thread

Enough narrow ribbon to go around the top and base of your lampshade

Fast-drying craft glue

2. Arrange the ruffles evenly along the length of the ribbon and machine stitch along the centre of the ribbon.

3. Pin and machine stitch a length of narrow ribbon over the stitching on the ruffled ribbon.

4. Glue the ruffled ribbon around the bottom of the lampshade, overlapping the ends neatly to finish. Glue narrow ribbon around the top of the lampshade, starting and finishing at the same spot as the bottom ruffle.

Simple curtain with patterned border

Liven up a plain curtain with patterned borders and braids or use this method to lengthen existing curtains to fit a new window. Choose fabrics with similar colours, mixing spots, stripes and florals, and add ricrac braid and ribbon for extra decoration.

3 hours

YOU WILL NEED

Spotted fabric
50 cm/20 in. striped fabric
50 cm/20 in. floral fabric
Sewing machine and matching thread
Two lengths of braid
One length of jumbo ricrac braid
Curtain lining fabric
Curtain heading tape

Take 1.5-cm/1/2-in. seam allowances throughout unless otherwise stated.

1. Cut a piece of spotted fabric to the required size. Cut a piece of striped fabric 26 cm/10¼ in. deep and a piece of floral fabric 29 cm/11½ in. deep; both pieces should be the same width as the spotted fabric. With right sides together, pin and machine stitch the striped fabric to the bottom of the spotted fabric and the floral fabric to the bottom of the striped fabric. Press open the seams.

2. Pin and machine stitch one piece of braid over the join between the floral and striped fabrics. Pin and stitch the ricrac braid along the join between the striped and spotted fabrics. Lay the second piece of braid over half of the ricrac and stitch in place.

3. Cut a piece of lining fabric the same length as the curtain and 3 cm/1¼ in. narrower. With right sides together, pin and machine stitch the lining fabric to the curtain along both long sides. Turn right side out and press.

4. At the top of the curtain, turn over 1 cm/3⁄8 in. to the wrong side. Turn over an additional 5 cm/2 in. and pin. Pin the curtain heading tape along this folded section and machine stitch in place. Hem the bottom of the curtain by folding over 1 cm/3⁄8 in. and another 3 cm/1¼ in. and machine stitch in place.

Curtain tieback

2 hours

Template on page 167

Tracing paper, pencil and pattern for paper

25 cm/10 in. natural linen

25 cm/10 in. iron-on interfacing

75-cm/30-in. length of 2.5-cm-/1-in.-wide ribbon

150 cm/60 in. braid

12 x 22-mm/^{7}/$_8$-in. self-cover buttons

25 cm/10 in. spotted fabric

Scraps of fabric to cover buttons

Sewing machine and matching thread

Take 1.5-cm/^{1}/$_2$-in. seam allowances throughout unless otherwise stated.

Tiebacks can be a decorative feature in their own right as well as a means of holding curtains out of the way when they are not in use. Make this one from a plain fabric that is used elsewhere in the room and then add simple fabric rosettes, each with a button covered in patterned fabric, at the centre, to provide little splashes of colour.

1. Enlarge the template on page 167 by 360%, trace it onto pattern paper and cut out. Pin the pattern onto a double thickness of natural linen fabric. Cut out.

2. Using the paper pattern, cut out one piece of iron-on interfacing and iron it onto the wrong side of one linen piece. Place one linen piece right side up, with a length of ribbon at either end. Place the other linen piece right side down on top and machine stitch together, leaving an opening of about 8 cm/3 in. in one side. Snip around the seam allowance.

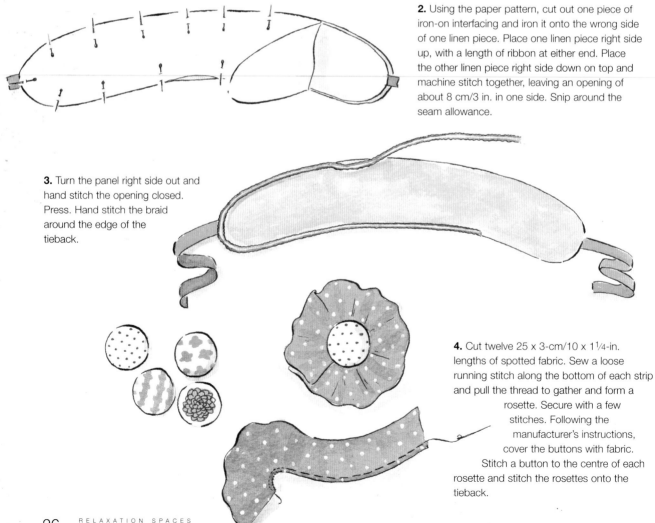

3. Turn the panel right side out and hand stitch the opening closed. Press. Hand stitch the braid around the edge of the tieback.

4. Cut twelve 25 x 3-cm/10 x 1^1/$_4$-in. lengths of spotted fabric. Sew a loose running stitch along the bottom of each strip and pull the thread to gather and form a rosette. Secure with a few stitches. Following the manufacturer's instructions, cover the buttons with fabric. Stitch a button to the centre of each rosette and stitch the rosettes onto the tieback.

Fireplace screen

This little three-panel screen is ideal for covering an open fireplace or for hiding ugly radiators or electricity sockets. The addition of a pretty fabric-and-ribbon flower makes it a lovely decorative item in its own right. You can increase the size of the panels to make a room screen or add more panels to cover a wider area.

2½ hours

3 pieces of 15-mm/½-in. MDF measuring 22 x 70 cm/ 8½ x 28 in.

150 cm/60 in. fabric

550 cm/6 yd ribbon plus 150 cm/60 in. for the flower

Fast-drying craft glue

4 small hinges

Bradawl

Screwdriver

Spray adhesive

Paper for pattern

Button

Needle and thread

1. Cut a piece of fabric measuring 54 x 64 cm/18 x 28¾ in. Apply spray adhesive to both sides of one of the MDF panels and lay the panel on the wrong side of the fabric, leaving 1.5 cm/½ in. of fabric around three sides of the panel and making sure there are no wrinkles in the fabric.

3. Glue around the edges of the panel as before, and stick the fabric onto it, again ensuring that the finish is smooth. Repeat Steps 1–3 with the other two panels of MDF.

2. Apply a thin line of craft glue around the three sides of the MDF and stick the fabric onto it, folding the corners neatly. Turn the panel over and press the fabric onto the other side, smoothing the fabric to remove any creases or air bubbles.

4. Mark the positions for the hinges along the edges of the panels and make holes with a bradawl. Screw the hinges in place so that the three panels are connected.

5. Apply a thin layer of glue along the edges of the panels and glue the ribbon in place, overlapping the ends of the ribbon slightly at what will be the bottom of the screen.

6. Cut six 23-cm/9-in. lengths of ribbon. Form each one into a loop, overlapping the ends a little in the middle, and work a few stitches by hand to hold in place. Stitch all six loops together in the middle to form a flower.

7. Measure a strip of fabric 35 x 5 cm/14 x 2 in. and tear it off the main piece. Work a line of running stitches (see page 163) along one long edge and pull the thread to gather the strip into a rosette, securing the end with a few small stitches. Hand stitch the ribbon-loop flower made in Step 6 to the back of the rosette.

8. Sew a button onto the centre of the fabric-and-ribbon flower and sew it in place on the front panel of the screen. Finish with a few tight stitches to hold the flower securely in place.

CHAPTER 2

Kitchens and dining rooms

Tea cosy

2½ hours

Keep tea piping hot with this vintage-feel tea cosy. The combination of gingham and floral fabrics, edged with pretty braids, is a surefire winner. You could easily make a taller cosy to fit a coffee pot – or for a cute, homely feel, why not try making miniature versions from little scraps of fabric to cover your breakfast boiled eggs?

YOU WILL NEED

Template on page 167
Tracing paper and pencil
50 cm/20 in. pink fabric
50 cm/20 in. gingham fabric
50 cm/20 in. floral fabric
75 cm/30 in. gingham ribbon
75 cm/30 in. floral trim
50 cm/20 in. medium-weight wadding
Sewing machine and matching sewing thread

Take 1.5-cm/½-in. seam allowances throughout unless otherwise stated.

1. Using the template on page 167, cut two pieces of pink fabric. Cut a panel of gingham measuring 19.5 x 27 cm/7¾ x 10¾ in. Fold over 1 cm/³⁄₈ in. to the wrong side along both long sides of the gingham and press. (Use the lines of the gingham as a guide, to get a straight edge.) Centre the gingham panel on the front of one of the pink fabric pieces and machine stitch it in place. Trim off any excess gingham, following the curve of the pink fabric.

2. Cut a piece of floral fabric measuring 9 x 27 cm/3 x 10¾ in. and fold under both long edges by 1.5 cm/½ in. Pin the floral fabric centrally onto the gingham fabric, slipping a length of gingham ribbon under both edges. Machine stitch through all layers. Stitch a length of floral trim along both edges of the gingham fabric.

3. To make the hanging loop, cut a 3.5 x 5-cm/1½ x 2-in. piece of floral fabric. Fold over each long side by 1 cm/³⁄₈ in., and then fold in half lengthways and machine stitch along the folded edges. Press. Using the template, cut two pieces of medium-weight wadding. Lay one piece on your work surface, with the front of the tea cosy right side up on top, and pin the hanging loop to the centre of the curved side. Lay the back of the tea cosy right side down on top, followed by a piece of wadding. Machine stitch all around the curved edge.

4. Using the template, cut two pieces of gingham. Machine stitch around the curved side, leaving a 20-cm/8-in. gap along the top. Put the gingham over the front of the tea cosy, right sides together. Stitch together around the bottom. Turn right side out and hand stitch the opening closed on the gingham fabric.

Cutlery roll

2 hours

This is the perfect way to store a set of cutlery, to prevent the individual pieces from getting scratched and keep all the components together. Alternatively, use it to keep picnic cutlery handy for *al fresco* dining so that you're always ready for an impromptu summer outing. Careful measuring is essential, to ensure that the compartments are evenly spaced across the roll.

YOU WILL NEED

50 cm/20 in. patterned fabric

50 cm/20 in. polka-dot fabric

86-cm/34-in. length of 22-mm-/1-in.-wide grosgrain ribbon

Sewing machine

Needle and matching sewing thread

Take 1.5-cm/$^{1}/_{2}$-in. seam allowances throughout unless otherwise stated.

1. Cut a 62 x 12-cm/24$^{1}/_{2}$ x 4$^{3}/_{4}$-in. rectangle of polka-dot fabric and a 62 x 6-cm/24$^{1}/_{2}$ x 2$^{1}/_{4}$-in. strip of patterned fabric. With right sides together, aligning raw edges, lay the patterned fabric along one long edge of the polka-dot strip and machine stitch 1.5 cm/$^{1}/_{2}$ in. in from the edge. Fold the patterned strip over, turn under and press 1.5 cm/$^{1}/_{2}$ in. along the remaining raw edge, and slipstitch in place along the back.

2. Cut a 62 x 33-cm/24$^{1}/_{2}$ x 13-in. rectangle of polka-dot fabric. Lay the patterned border piece along one long edge, with the raw edges together at the bottom. Measure 6 cm/2$^{1}/_{4}$ in. in from one side and pin from the top to the bottom of the smaller panel. Continue along the panel, pinning every 5 cm/2 in. There will be another 6-cm/2$^{1}/_{4}$-in. pocket at the other end. Machine stitch along each pinned line.

3. Cut an 86-cm/34-in. length of blue grosgrain ribbon. Cut a 67 x 39-cm/26$^{1}/_{4}$ x 15$^{1}/_{4}$-in. piece of patterned fabric. Pin the ribbon across the fabric 13 cm/5 in. from the bottom and 3.5 cm/1$^{1}/_{2}$ in. from the edge, leaving the same amount of ribbon extending beyond each edge. Machine stitch the ribbon onto the fabric, stitching a rectangle 12 cm/4$^{3}/_{4}$ in. long to fix the ribbon securely in place.

4. With wrong sides together, centre the polka-dot panel on the patterned fabric, leaving an even border all the way around. Fold the corners over and fold each side of the patterned fabric over by 1 cm/⅜ in. and then by another 1.5 cm/½ in. Pin, tack and machine stitch in place, stitching as close to the folded edge as possible.

1. Cut an 18 x 25-cm/7 x 10-in. piece of patterned fabric and two 6.5 x 25-cm/2½ x 10-in. pieces of plain fabric. With right sides together, lay each plain piece along one long side of the patterned piece. Pin and machine stitch together. Press the seams open.

Pan holder

This practical pan holder is very straightforward to make and requires only limited sewing skills. Choose a bold pattern for a striking look and line with thick wadding to provide adequate protection from the heat. Hang it up by the fabric loop and it will always be on hand when you need it.

1½ hours

2. Cut two 26-cm/10¼-in. squares of thick wadding. Place the backing fabric wrong side up on your work surface, with the wadding squares on top and the front of the cover right side up on top of the wadding. Pin all layers together. Stick a piece of masking tape diagonally from one corner to the other and machine stitch along the edge of the tape. Reposition the tape 3 cm/1¼ in. from the stitching line. Stitch along the edge. Continue until you reach the corner. Lay masking tape across the other two corners and repeat the stitching process until the whole mat is quilted.

3. Cut a piece of fabric on the bias 100 cm/40 in. long and 4 cm/1½ in. wide. (Join several pieces together if necessary.) With right sides together, pin it all around the right side of the mat, aligning the raw edges. Fold under the end for a neat finish and machine stitch in place. Trim the corners.

4. To make the hanging loop, cut an 18 x 5-cm/7 x 2-in. strip of patterned fabric. Fold over the long edges by 1 cm/³⁄₈ in. and then fold in half lengthways. Machine stitch, stitching as close to the edge as possible. Fold the bias strip over to the back of the mat and turn under 1 cm/³⁄₈ in. Pin, then slipstitch to the mat all the way around, centring the loop on one side.

Place mat and napkin

Add a touch of elegance to your dinner table with these smart place mats and matching napkins. Quick and easy to make, they would be an ideal wedding or housewarming gift that the recipients will treasure for many years to come.

As table linen requires regular laundering, make sure you wash all the fabrics before you start sewing so that there's no risk of them shrinking once the project is finished.

Placemat: 1 hour
Napkin: 20 minutes

YOU WILL NEED

For each place mat:
50 cm/20 in. patterned fabric

50 cm/20 in. gingham fabric

50 cm/20 in. plain fabric

50 cm/20 in. medium-weight iron-on interfacing

For each napkin:
50 cm/20 in. patterned fabric

50 cm/20 in. gingham fabric

Sewing machine

Needle and matching sewing thread

Take 1.5-cm/^{1}/$_2$-in. seam allowances throughout unless otherwise stated.

TO MAKE THE PLACE MATS

1. For each place mat, cut a 34 x 26-cm/13^1/$_2$ x 10-in. rectangle of plain fabric, two 34 x 12-cm/13^1/$_2$ x 4^1/$_2$-in. rectangles of patterned fabric and two 34 x 6-cm/13^1/$_2$ x 2^1/$_4$-in. rectangles of gingham fabric. With right sides together, machine stitch one gingham piece along each long side of the plain fabric, then machine stitch one patterned piece to the other long side of each gingham piece. Press the seams open.

2. Cut a 34 x 50-cm/13^1/$_2$ x 19^1/$_2$-in. piece of interfacing. Lay the interfacing on the wrong side of the fabric panel, with the rough side down. Place a damp cloth on top and iron with a medium iron to fuse the interfacing to the fabric.

3. For the backing, cut a piece of gingham and a piece of interfacing, each measuring 34 x 50 cm/13^1/$_2$ x 19^1/$_2$ in. Iron the interfacing to the reverse of the gingham, as before. Lay the front of the mat right side up on your work surface with the back piece on top, right side down. Machine stitch all around the edge, leaving a gap of about 10 cm/4 in. in one side. Trim the corners. Turn right side out and hand stitch the opening closed. Press. Machine topstitch all around the edges.

TO MAKE THE NAPKINS

For each napkin, cut a 40-cm/16-in. square of patterned fabric and a 40-cm/16-in. square of gingham fabric. With right sides together, machine stitch all around, leaving a gap of about 10 cm/4 in. in one side. Trim the corners. Turn right side out and hand stitch the opening closed. Press. Machine topstitch all around the edges, 2.5 cm/1 in. from the edge.

Napkin ring
with button detail

Scraps of leftover fabric can be put to brilliant use in these charming napkin rings. The ends of each ring are stitched together and decorated with a single button – a great way of adding a pretty little finishing detail without having to go to the bother of stitching a buttonhole.

45 minutes

YOU WILL NEED

25 cm/10 in. patterned fabric
25 cm/10 in. plain fabric
50 cm/20 in. ricrac braid
50 cm/20 in. narrow gingham ribbon
Sewing machine
Needle and matching sewing thread
Button approx. 2 cm/³/4 in. in diameter

Take 1.5-cm/¹/2-in. seam allowances throughout unless otherwise stated.

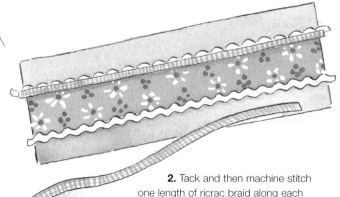

1. For each napkin ring, cut a 4 x 23-cm/ 1¹/2 x 9-in. rectangle of patterned fabric and two 8.5 x 23-cm/3¹/4 x 9-in. rectangles of plain fabric. Centre the patterned fabric on top of one of the plain pieces and tack in place (see page 163).

2. Tack and then machine stitch one length of ricrac braid along each long edge of the patterned fabric. Tack and then machine stitch one length of ribbon over the edge of each length of ricrac, leaving half the ricrac visible. Remove all the tacking stitches.

3. With right sides together, pin and tack the decorated strip of fabric and the remaining plain piece together. Machine stitch along three sides, leaving one short end open. Remove the tacking stitches. Trim the seam allowance, turn right side out and press. Fold in the open end of the napkin ring by 1.5 cm/½ in. and slipstitch closed (see page 163).

4. Overlap the short ends of the strip by about 2.5 cm/1 in. and stitch a button in place, stitching through all layers.

Fringed tablecloth with braid

This fabulously floral tablecloth is extremely easy to make – and will add a burst of colour to any room. Simply stitch fringed braid around a hemmed square of fabric and add a pretty ribbon with little bows to finish.

<table>
<tr><td>1½ hours</td></tr>
</table>

YOU WILL NEED

Floral fabric

Cotton fringing

Thin ribbon

Sewing machine and matching sewing thread

Take 1.5-cm/½-in. seam allowances throughout unless otherwise stated.

1. Cut a piece of floral fabric to fit your table, adding about 30 cm/12 in. on all sides for the overhang and 2.5 cm/1 in. for the hem. Fold over 1 cm/³⁄8 in. and another 1.5 cm/½ in. to the wrong side all the way around. Pin and machine stitch in place. Press.

2. Pin the fringing all the way around the edge of the fabric and machine stitch it in place, folding the end under for a neat finish.

3. Pin and machine stitch the ribbon along the top of the fringing, again folding the end under slightly. Tie eight small ribbon bows. Hand stitch one to each corner and one centrally along each side.

Table runner

A table runner can add the finishing touch to a dinner table. This easy-to-stitch runner is made from a bold, modern fabric and will work equally well laid on top of a plain-coloured tablecloth or straight onto the table for a more informal look. If there is no obvious lengthways pattern, you can economise on fabric by cutting the fabric across the width, joining two widths together to make a long strip if necessary.

| 1½ hours |

YOU WILL NEED

Patterned fabric
Plain fabric
Sewing machine and matching sewing thread
Needle and thread
6 self-cover buttons 5 cm/2 in. in diameter

Take 1.5-cm/½-in. seam allowances throughout unless otherwise stated.

1. Decide how long you want the runner to be. Cut two pieces of patterned fabric 3 cm/1¼ in. longer than this measurement and 33 cm/13 in. wide.

2. Cut two pieces of plain fabric the same length as the patterned fabric and 11 cm/ 4 in. wide. With right sides together, pin and machine stitch one plain piece along each side of one of the patterned pieces. Press the seams open.

3. With right sides together, pin and machine stitch the second piece of patterned fabric to the remaining raw edges of the plain fabric pieces to form a tube. Carefully press the seams open.

4. Pin across the short ends of the runner, making sure that the seams of the patterned fabrics align and that you have an even-sized border of plain fabric on each side. Machine stitch along one short end of the runner and turn right side out.

5. Turn under 1.5 cm/½ in. on the open end of the runner and hand stitch closed. Press carefully.

6. Following the manufacturer's instructions, cover the buttons with patterned fabric. Hand stitch three buttons to each end of the runner, spacing them evenly across the patterned fabric.

Recipe book cover

2 hours

Keep all your recipes together in this pretty but practical book. I used fabric with an old-fashioned feel and maintained the nostalgic theme by using a vintage button and ties to hold everything in place, while a ribbon stitched into the lining makes a handy bookmarker.

WORKING OUT FABRIC QUANTITIES

To work out the depth of each fabric strip, measure from the top to the bottom of the book that you want to cover, add 4 cm/1½ in. and divide by three. To work out the length of each fabric strip, measure across the back, spine and front of the book and add 15 cm/6 in.

YOU WILL NEED

Notebook
25 cm/10 in. of three floral fabrics
25 cm/10 in. gingham fabric for the lining
25 cm/10 in. medium-weight iron-on interfacing
Sewing machine and matching sewing thread
Length of 12-mm/½-in. ribbon for bookmark
30-cm/12-in. length of 15-mm/⅝-in. ribbon for ties
Square button 2.5 cm/1 in. in diameter

Take 1.5-cm/½-in. seam allowances throughout unless otherwise stated.

1. Cut three strips of floral fabric to the required size. With right sides together, pin and machine stitch the strips together. Press the seams open.

2. Cut a piece of gingham fabric and a piece of interfacing the same size as the floral piece. Using a damp cloth, iron the interfacing to the back of the gingham.

3. Place the floral piece right side up on your work surface. For the bookmark, cut a piece of narrow ribbon 5 cm/2 in. longer than the book and pin it centrally along one long edge. Place the lining piece wrong side up on top. Pin and machine stitch together, leaving an opening of about 7 cm/3 in. along one side. Trim the corners, turn right side out and press. Hand stitch the opening closed.

4. Fold over the side edges by 5.5 cm/2¼ in. and pin. Check that the cover fits the notebook snugly. Top stitch all around. Cut two 15-cm/6-in. lengths of 15-mm/⅝-in. ribbon for the ties. Stitch one to the front of the book and one to the back and finish with a button on the front, making sure that you only stitch through the top layer of the cover.

CHAPTER 3

Bedrooms

Reversible duvet cover

Choose bold, contemporary fabrics for this reversible duvet cover. It can be difficult to buy fabric that is wide enough to fit a double bed, especially if you're using a fabric with a large pattern, so joining squares of fabric together is the perfect solution. The backing is made from two lengths of fabric stitched together to make the required width.

3 hours

1. Cut eight 53-cm/20¾-in. squares of each of the two patterned fabrics.

YOU WILL NEED

225 cm/90 in. each of 2 co-ordinating patterned fabrics

450 cm/180 in. striped fabric

Sewing machine and matching sewing thread

Take 1.5-cm/½-in. seam allowances throughout unless otherwise stated.

2. With right sides together, alternating the fabrics, pin and machine stitch the squares together to form four rows of four squares each. Press the seams open.

3. With right sides together, pin and machine stitch the four patchwork rows together to make a block of 16 squares. Press the seams open.

4. Cut two pieces of striped fabric 203 cm/80 in. long and the full width of the fabric. Cut off one of the selvedges on each piece. With right sides together, pin and machine stitch the pieces together along the cut edges. Press the seam open. Place the fabric on your work surface. Measure 101.5 cm/40 in. either side of the centre seam and use tailor's chalk to draw a line the full length of the fabric. Cut the fabric along these lines to a width of 203 cm/80 in.

5. Measure 71.5cm/28 in. from one corner of the patchwork panel and make a cut 1.5 cm/1/2 in. deep. Repeat from the other corner of the same edge of the panel. Press the central section to the wrong side by 5 mm/1/4 in. and then turn this over by another 1 cm/3/8 in. Pin and machine stitch along the folded-over section. Repeat on the striped panel of fabric.

7. Snip the corners of the seam allowance off, turn right side out and press.

6. With right sides together, pin the front of the duvet cover to the back piece. Machine stitch from the stitched section at the bottom all the way around to the other end of the stitched section.

Sheet with ribbon trim

There is nothing more inviting than fresh, cotton bed linen. Embroidered and hand-decorated linens can be expensive, so cheat by sewing pretty ribbons along the top edge of a shop-bought sheet. Stitch ribbons onto pillowcases to complete the look, using colours that co-ordinate with the décor of the room.

45 minutes

YOU WILL NEED

White sheet

Three co-ordinating lengths of ribbon 1 cm/3⁄8 in., 1.5 cm/ 1⁄2 in. and 3 cm/1 1⁄4 in. in width

Sewing machine and matching sewing thread

1. Measure the sheet and cut a length of 1.5-cm/1⁄2-in. ribbon about 5 cm/ 2 in. longer than the width of the sheet. Pin the ribbon along the top of the sheet 1.5 cm/1⁄2 in. from the edge, folding under 2.5 cm/1 in. at each end. Measure from the edge of the sheet to the ribbon as you work to ensure that it's straight. Machine stitch in place.

2. Following Step 1, cut a length of the 3-cm/1 1⁄4-in. ribbon, pin it across the sheet 5 mm/1⁄4 in. below the first, and machine stitch in place.

3. Pin the narrowest ribbon across the sheet, 1.5 cm/1⁄2 in. below the second ribbon, and machine stitch as before.

Pillowcase with patterned border

Make crisp, white cotton pillowcases even more appealing by adding a decorative fabric border. You could use the same fabric to edge sheets, as well – a simple way to create a really special wedding or housewarming gift.

YOU WILL NEED

75 cm/30 in. patterned fabric
25 cm/10 in. plain fabric
50 cm/20 in. of 5 mm/¼ in. ribbon
125 cm/50 in. white fabric
Sewing machine
Matching sewing thread
Needle

Take 1.5-cm/½-in. seam allowances throughout unless otherwise stated.

1. Cut a 53 x 41-cm/21 x 16-in. piece of patterned fabric and two 53 x 7-cm/21 x 3-in. pieces of plain fabric. With right sides together, aligning the raw edges, lay one plain strip along each long side of the patterned fabric. Pin and machine stitch in place. Press the seams open. Pin and stitch the ribbon over one of the seams.

2. Cut a 53 x 54-cm/21 x 21¼-in. piece of white fabric. With right sides together, pin and stitch the border piece onto the white fabric, with the ribbon-edged plain piece closest to this seam. Press the seam towards the border piece.

3. At the other end of the border, fold over 1.5 cm/½ in. to the wrong side and press. With wrong sides together, fold the border back on itself and hand stitch in place, aligning the folded edge with the edge of the border on the front. Press.

4. Cut a 53 x 98-cm/21 x 38½-in. piece of white fabric. Along one short end, fold over 1 cm/⅜ in. and then another 1.5 cm/½ in. Machine stitch, stitching as close to the edge as possible. Lay the piece right side up on your work surface. Lay the front of the cover right side down on top, aligning the raw edges. Fold the hemmed flap of white fabric over the front of the cover. Pin and machine stitch along the short raw end and both long sides. Trim the seams and turn right side out. Press.

Little girl's duvet set

Surprisingly simple to make, this pretty bed linen set in shades of girly pink will fit perfectly into any little princess's bedroom. Simply stitch two strips of co-ordinating fabric to either side of a panel of floral fabric to create a lovely patchwork effect, and finish with ties on the pillowcase and duvet cover. The key with this design is to use small-print fabrics for the co-ordinating fabrics, as this allows the bold floral design in the centre to really make an impact.

YOU WILL NEED

For the duvet cover:

75 cm/30 in. each of two co-ordinating fabrics, 150 cm/59 in. wide

125 cm/50 in. floral fabric, 150 cm/59 in. wide

250 cm/100 in. backing fabric, 150 cm/59 in. wide

For the pillowcase:

75 cm/30 in. each of two co-ordinating fabrics, 150 cm/59 in. wide

75 cm/30 in. floral fabric, 150 cm/59 in. wide

75 cm/30 in. backing fabric, 150 cm/59 in. wide

Sewing machine

Matching sewing thread

Take 1.5-cm/1/2-in. seam allowances throughout unless otherwise stated.

TO MAKE THE DUVET COVER

1. Cut two 25 x 138-cm/10 x 54 1/2-in. pieces of each of the co-ordinating border fabrics. With right sides together, pin and machine stitch one piece of each fabric together along one long side to make the border pieces. Press the seams open.

2. Cut an 111 x 138-cm/43 3/4 x 54 1/2-in. rectangle of floral fabric. With right sides together, pin and machine stitch one border piece to each end. Press the seams open.

3. To make the ties, cut six 36 x 5-cm/14 x 2-in. pieces of one of the co-ordinating fabrics. Along each long side of each tie, fold over 1 cm/3/8 in. to the wrong side. Fold over 1 cm/3/8 in. at one short end of each tie. Fold each tie in half lengthways and stitch, stitching as close to the edge as possible.

4. Cut a 203 x 138-cm/80 x 54½-in. rectangle of fabric for the back of the duvet cover. Pin three ties along one short end of the fabric on the right side, spacing them evenly. Cut a 39 x 138-cm/15½ x 54½-in. strip of the backing fabric for the flap. Along one long edge, fold over 1 cm/³/₈ in. and then another 1.5 cm/½ in. to the wrong side and machine stitch. With right sides together, aligning the raw edges, pin this strip on the backing fabric and machine stitch along the top, sandwiching the ties in between.

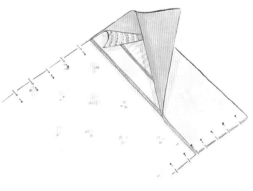

5. Along one short end of the front of the cover, fold over 1.5 cm/½ in. and then another 1.5 cm/½ in. to the wrong side. Place the raw ends of the remaining strips under the fold, spacing them as for the back piece, and machine stitch along the fold. Flip the ties over so that they hang off the bottom of the fabric and work a few stitches to keep them in place.

6. Lay the back piece on your work surface, right side up. Place the front piece on top, right side down, aligning the raw edges. Fold the flap on the back piece over the front piece. Pin and stitch along both long sides of the cover and the raw short side. Trim the corners and turn right side out. Press.

TO MAKE THE PILLOWCASE

1. Cut two 53 x 12-cm/20¾ x 4¾-in. rectangles of each of the co-ordinating border fabrics. With right sides together, pin and machine stitch one piece of each fabric together along one long side. Press the seams open. Cut a 41 x 53-cm/16 x 20¾-in. rectangle of floral fabric. Pin and machine stitch one border piece to each long end. Press the seams open.

2. Make four ties, as in Step 3 of the duvet cover. Attach two ties to the front of the pillowcase, as in Step 5 of the duvet cover.

3. Cut a 78 x 53-cm/30¾ x 20¾-in. piece of fabric for the back of the pillowcase and a 19 x 53-cm/7½ x 20¾-in. piece for the flap. Hem one long side of the flap, as in Step 4 of the duvet cover. Lay the back piece right side up on your work surface. Place the two remaining ties on top, spacing them as for the front piece. Place the hemmed flap right side down on top, aligning the raw edges, and machine stitch. Follow Step 6 of the duvet cover to sew the pillowcase together.

Patchwork bedspread

This colourful patchwork quilt, made from pretty floral and polka-dot fabrics, uses large, machine-sewn squares of fabric – a time-saving way to create a bedspread with a homespun feel. Remember, when you're making patchwork it's important to use fabrics of similar weights.

For this design, choose fabrics with similar colours, adding a few contrasting patterns for a fresh, modern look. Finish off the quilt with a ribbon border and stitch on an assortment of buttons which, as well as providing a decorative touch, hold the layers of the quilt together.

YOU WILL NEED

50 cm/20 in. each of six cotton fabrics
Pattern paper
150 cm/60 in. backing fabric
150 cm/60 in. lightweight wadding
Sewing machine
Needle and matching sewing threads
490-cm/192-in. length of ribbon
Assorted buttons

Take 1.5-cm/½-in. seam allowances throughout unless otherwise stated.

1. Cut a 19-cm/7½-in. square piece of paper to use as a pattern. Cut out squares from a range of different fabrics by folding the fabrics over concertina style and laying the pattern piece on top, so that you can cut squares from several layers at once. You will need 54 squares in total.

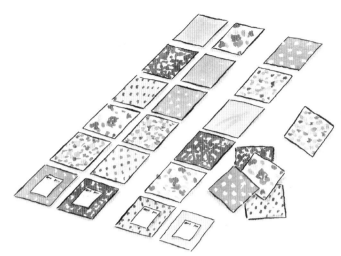

2. Lay the fabric squares out on your work surface in six rows of nine squares each and move them around until you have a pleasing arrangement, making sure that no two squares of the same fabric are next to each other. Pin a paper label onto each row of squares, numbered from 1 to 9.

3. Starting with row 1, pin and machine stitch the squares together. Press open the seams. Repeat with the remaining eight rows of squares.

4. Lay the strips on your work surface in the correct order. Pin and machine stitch them together, aligning the seams, and press the seams open. Remove the paper labels.

5. Lay the backing fabric on your work surface, with the wadding on top and the patchwork panel on top of the wadding. Pin all the layers together and cut the wadding and backing to the same size as the patchwork. Remove the pins.

6. Place the backing fabric to one side. Pin and tack the patchwork panel to the wadding. Work from the centre outwards, pinning in a diagonal line out to each corner, and then in a straight line from the centre to the centre of each side.

7. Lay the patchwork and wadding panel right side up on your work surface, with the backing fabric right side down on top. Pin through all layers, working from the centre outwards as in Step 6. Machine stitch, leaving a 30-cm/12-in. opening at one end. Snip the corners and trim the seam allowance a little.

8. Turn the quilt right side out and press. Hand stitch the opening closed. Pin, tack and machine stitch the ribbon onto the top of the quilt, about 1.5 cm/1/2 in. in from the edge all the way around. Mitre the corners for a neat finish. Turn the end of the ribbon under a little and stitch to finish.

9. Hand stitch buttons onto the quilt, making sure that the stitches go through all layers of the quilt. Use a selection of buttons in a random arrangement.

Bolster

2 hours

This bolster, made from a very striking Chinese-style fabric, would be an attractive and useful cushion for a bed. The main panel of fabric is twinned with a striped fabric in the same colours, while a coordinating ribbon in a bold contemporary polka-dot design adds a smart finishing touch. Simple fabric ties hold the bolster cover closed; with no complicated fastenings to worry about, this is a really speedy project to create! To speed things up even further, you could replace the ties with wide, plain-coloured ribbons.

YOU WILL NEED

57 cm/22½ in. patterned fabric
65 cm/25½ in. striped fabric
115-cm/45-in. length of 1-cm/³⁄₈-in. ribbon
Bolster 48 cm/19 in. long

Take 1.5-cm/½-in. seam allowances throughout unless otherwise stated.

1. Cut one 41 x 57-cm/16 x 22½-in. piece of patterned fabric and two 65 x 57-cm/25½ x 221½-in. pieces of striped fabric. With right sides together, machine stitch one piece of striped fabric along each long edge of the patterned fabric. Press the seams open. On the right side of the fabric, machine stitch a length of ribbon over each seam. Press.

2. With right sides together, fold the fabric in half lengthways, aligning the raw edges. Pin and machine stitch along the raw edge. Press

3. At each short end of the bolster cover, fold over 1.5 cm/½ in. of fabric and press. Fold the striped fabric back level with the seam between the striped and patterned fabrics and hand stitch the folded edges to the seam. Turn the cover right side out and press.

4. For the ties, cut two 52 x 9-cm/20½ x 3½-in. pieces of patterned fabric. Fold over 1.5 cm/½ in. to the wrong side along each short edge and press. Do the same along each long edge and press. Fold in half lengthways, aligning the folded edges, and press. Machine stitch, stitching as close to the edge as possible, and press. Pull the cover over the bolster and tie one tie neatly around each end.

Piece of MDF 15 mm/⅝ in. thick, measuring 60 cm/24 in. high x the width of the bed
Drill and bit
Thick wadding
Fast-drying craft glue
Polka-dot fabric
Ricrac braid
4 x 4-cm/1½-in. self-cover buttons
25 cm/10 in. fabric to cover the buttons
4 x 2-cm/¾-in. plain buttons
150 cm/60 in. gingham ribbon 22 mm/⅞ in. wide
Needle and upholstery thread
Two pieces of 5 x 2.5-cm/2 x 1-in. wood for legs (the length depends on required height of the bedhead)

WORKING OUT FABRIC QUANTITIES

For the polka-dot fabric, allow twice the size of the headboard plus 25 cm/10 in. For the ricrac braid, you will need twice the width and four times the height of the board. Finally, cut a piece of wadding the same size as the headboard.

Padded headboard

3 hours

This padded headboard requires only a little very simple sewing and is surprisingly easy to construct. The headboard is padded with a layer of wadding and covered with a cheery polka-dot fabric. The buttons are covered with bits of embroidery cut from old tablecloths that have seen better days – but you could use any scraps of fabric. Two rows of ricrac braid finish the board off beautifully.

1. Divide the width of the headboard by 5. Measure this distance down from the top of the headboard, and then measure and mark the same distance at intervals across the board. Drill a hole at each marked point.

2. Cut a piece of wadding to fit the front of the board. Apply glue to the board and stick the wadding in place.

3. Add 25 cm/10 in. to the width and 25 cm/10 in. to the height of the board and cut a piece of polka-dot fabric to this size. On the right side of the fabric, pin and machine stitch ricrac braid around both short ends and along one long side of the fabric 11 cm/4½ in. from the edge. Pin and machine stitch a second length of ricrac braid about 5 mm/¼ in. from the first.

4. Press the fabric and then lay it centrally on the front of the headboard. Pull the excess fabric over to the back of the board and glue it in place, folding the corners neatly. Make sure that the fabric on the front of the headboard is crease free.

5. Cut a piece of polka-dot fabric 4 cm/1½ in. bigger all around than the headboard. Fold over 5 cm/2 in. to the wrong side all the way around and press. Glue the fabric to the back of the headboard, smoothing it in place.

6. Following the manufacturer's instructions, cover the buttons with fabric. Cut four 35-cm/14-in. lengths of gingham ribbon. Work running stitch along one edge of each one and pull the thread to gather the ribbon into a rosette. Place each rosette in turn behind a covered button to make sure that it is the correct size and then finish with a few small stitches to hold the rosette shape.

7. Thread an upholstery needle, knotting the end of the thread. Take the needle through one of the plain buttons. Working from the back of the headboard, thread the needle through one of the holes in the board, pulling the thread all the way through so that the button sits tightly against the headboard. Take the needle through a ribbon rosette and then through one of the covered buttons. Stitch back through the hole in the headboard. Repeat until all four rosettes are in place.

8. Pull the thread to the back of the board and make a few stitches through the button, finishing with a few stitches on the fabric to secure the buttons in place. Cut two pieces of wood to the required length and screw them onto the back of the board with wood screws.

Flowery throw

about 20 minutes per flower

Brighten up a plain wool blanket with these striking fabric flowers finished with a selection of vintage buttons. Felt or other fabrics that do not fray could also be used. Stitch the flowers at the corners, or group them in clusters all over the throw. The flowers would also be great made into brooches or used as decorations for a hat or bag.

YOU WILL NEED

5 baby cord fabrics in different colours
50 cm/20 in. fusible webbing
Templates on page 169
Tracing paper, pencil and paper for pattern
Selection of buttons
Plain wool blanket
Needle and thread
Pinking shears

1. Following the manufacturer's instructions, iron fusible webbing onto the back of the coloured fabrics. Trace the templates on page 169 onto paper and cut paper patterns for the large and small petal shapes and the overall flower shape. Cut a paper circle 3 cm/1¼ in. in diameter. Draw around the petal shapes on the back of the fabrics and cut out. You will need eight large petals and five small ones for each flower.

2. Using a needle and thread, make a few small stitches at the pointed end of the petal shapes to gather them slightly. Stitch eight large petals together at the pointed ends to make a flower.

3. Stitch five small petal shapes together at the pointed ends, as before. Sew the small petals onto the centre of the large flower. Finish by adding a button in the centre. Using the paper patterns from Step 1, cut out the required number of flower shapes. Using pinking shears, cut a circle for the centre of each flower in a different colour of fabric. Sew a circle to the centre of each flower shape and add a button to the centre to complete.

4. Arrange the flowers on the blanket. When you are happy with the arrangement, hand stitch the flowers in place.

Round lampshade

Compass

Tracing paper, pencil and
pattern paper

25 cm/10 in. each of 4 fabrics in
pastel colours for the rosettes

25 cm/10 in. green fabric for the
leaf shapes

Needle and matching sewing
thread

Selection of buttons

Enough pompom fringe to go
around the bottom of the shade
plus 1 cm/3⁄8 in.

Enough 5-mm/1⁄4-in. ribbon to
go round the top of the shade
plus 1 cm/3⁄8 in.

Fast-drying craft glue

Flower-and-leaf lampshade   2½ hours

This is a great way of livening up a plain lampshade. Make fabric yo-yos into sweet little flowers by stitching a button to the centre and then simply glue them onto the shade with fabric leaf shapes to finish.

1. Using a compass, draw a 9-cm/3½-in. circle and a 6-cm/2½-in. circle on paper. Cut out the circles to use as patterns, then pin them onto your chosen fabrics and cut out the required number of each fabric in each size. Using a needle and thread, work a line of running stitch all around the edge of each circle, securing the thread at the beginning with a few small stitches. Pull the thread to gather the circle into a rosette.

2. Finish with a few small stitches to hold the rosette in place. Stitch a button to the centre of each rosette. Draw a leaf shape on paper, and cut out. Pin the leaf pattern to green fabric. Cut out one or two leaves for each flower.

3. Using fast-drying craft glue, stick pompom fringe all around the bottom of the shade, overlapping the ends slightly. Make sure that the fringe is straight before the glue dries. Starting and finishing at the same side of the shade as the pompom fringe, glue ribbon around the top of the shade.

4. Glue the fabric and ribbon rosettes onto the shade, holding them in place for a few seconds until they are firmly stuck. Apply a thin layer of glue to the back of the leaf shapes and glue them onto the shade, one or two per rosette.

Sheer curtain with ribbons

2½ hours

With so many lovely patterned sheer fabrics in the shops now, it is easy to make something practical that still makes a statement in a room. Here, I've used lengths of ribbons and braids to make a pretty border.

YOU WILL NEED

Sheer fabric

5 different ribbons and ricrac braid the width of the finished curtain plus 10 cm/4 in.

Sewing machine and matching sewing thread

1. Cut a piece of sheer fabric to the required size (see right). Arrange the ribbons and ricrac braid across the bottom of the fabric, leaving at least 4 cm/1½ in. below the first ribbon to allow for the hem. Pin, tack and machine stitch the ribbons and braid in place, and then trim the ends level with the edge of the fabric.

2. Along the sides of the curtain, turn over 1 cm/3/8 in. and then another 1.5 cm/1/2 in. to the wrong side and press. Pin and machine stitch in place.

WORKING OUT FABRIC QUANTITIES

If the curtain is to be pulled fairly taut on the pole, you will need to cut a piece of fabric that is 5 cm/2 in. wider and 5 cm/2 in. longer than the window. If you want the curtain to be slightly gathered, allow about 25% extra when calculating the width.

3. Work out how many ties you will need: the first and last ties should be positioned about 3 cm/1¼ in. from each side of the curtain and the remainder should be spaced about 16 cm/6½ in. apart. For each pair of ties, cut a 43 x 13-cm/17 x 5-in. piece of fabric. With right sides together, fold each piece of fabric in half and machine stitch along the length and across one short end. Turn right side out, press the raw end under by 1.5 cm/1/2 in. and hand stitch closed. Fold the ties in half and pin to the top of the right side of the curtain. Cut a piece of fabric the same width as the curtain and 8 cm/ 3 in. deep. With right sides together, pin it along the top of the curtain. Machine stitch in place.

4. Fold the fabric strip over to the wrong side of the curtain and press 1.5 cm/1/2 in. under along the remaining raw edges. Machine stitch the strip to the back of the curtain. At the bottom of the curtain, turn under 1 cm/3/8 in. and then another 1.5 cm/1/2 in. and machine stitch in place. Press.

CHAPTER 4

Work and play spaces

Drawstring toy bags

You can never have enough storage space for toys and these drawstring bags are both functional and pretty. Made from oddments of fabric sewn together and decorated with a cute fabric flower, you can simply throw toys in them at the end of the day and hang on a peg rail. They would work equally well for storing gym kit or ballet shoes.

YOU WILL NEED

25 cm/10 in. of three co-ordinating fabrics
50 cm/20 in. backing fabric
45 cm/18 in. of three co-ordinating ribbons
125 cm/50 in. cord
Sewing machine
Template on page 171
Needle and thread
Scraps of fabric
Button 3 cm/1¼ in. in diameter

Take 1.5-cm/½-in. seam allowances throughout unless otherwise stated.

1. Cut a 45 x 18-cm/17½ x 7-in. piece of each of the three co-ordinating fabrics. With right sides together, machine stitch them together along their long edges. Press the seams open. Machine stitch one ribbon over each seam on the right side. Press.

2. Cut a 48 x 45-cm/19 x 17½-in. piece of fabric for the back of the bag. With right sides together, machine stitch the front and back together, leaving 7 cm/2¾ in. unstitched at the top of one side. Turn back the unstitched part of the side edges, so that it's level with the stitching, and press. Trim the corners at the base of the bag to reduce bulk. Fold the top of the bag over by 1 cm/⅜ in. and again by 3 cm/1¼ in. Machine stitch close to the folded edge to create a channel, then turn the bag right side out.

3. Cut two 21-cm/8-in. lengths of ribbon and machine stitch together to create a double thickness. Stitch onto the middle of the back of the bag, just below the channel, folding the ends under by 1 cm/⅜ in. Thread the cord through the channel. Cut two 7 x 8-cm/2⅔ x 3-in. rectangles of fabric. With wrong sides together, fold each piece in half widthways and machine stitch along both sides. Turn right side out and turn under the top edge by 1 cm/⅜ in. Push the ends of the cord into this pocket and machine stitch along the top.

4. Using the template on page 171, cut two petal shapes from each of five different fabrics. Pin each pair together and machine stitch around the edge, leaving a small gap for turning. Turn right side out and make a few small stitches to gather at the end. Stitch the five petals together to form a flower, and hand stitch to the bag, with a button in the centre. Attach the tip of each petal to the bag by making a few small stitches at the back.

Lined storage basket 1½ hours

This fabric lining is practical as well as pretty, as it prevents delicate items from snagging on the wicker basket. The idea could also be used to line storage baskets for linens, clothing and even toys.

WORKING OUT FABRIC QUANTITIES

To work out how much fabric you need for the sides of the basket, measure around the top of the outside of the basket and add 3 cm/1¼ in. Then measure the height and add the amount that you want to fold over to the outside of the basket, plus 1.5 cm/½ in.

To work out how much fabric you need for the base of the basket, measure along one long edge and add 3 cm/1¼ in. Then measure along one short side and add 3 cm/1¼ in. to this measurement, too.

You will also need enough ribbon to go all around the top of the basket and the handles, plus 120 cm/48 in.

YOU WILL NEED

Patterned fabric

Ribbon 15 mm/½ in. wide

Sewing machine and matching sewing thread

Basket

Take 1.5-cm/½-in. seam allowances throughout unless otherwise stated.

1. Cut a strip of patterned fabric for the sides of the basket (see above). With right sides together, pin the ends together. Place the fabric inside the basket, wrong side out. Check that it fits snugly around the top of the basket and fold it over to make sure that the lining will not be too tight. Machine stitch the ends together and press the seam open.

2. Put the lining back into the basket, wrong side out, and press it into the corners with your fingers so that it fits snugly all around. Pin and tack any excess fabric at the corners to form a neat dart. Take the lining out of the basket and machine stitch the corners. (If the sides of your basket are straight, you can omit this step.)

3. Cut a rectangle of fabric for the base of the basket (see page 86). With right sides together, machine stitch the sides of the lining to the base. Trim the corners and press.

4. Place the lining inside the basket and mark where the handles are. Cut out a rectangle at each end that is exactly the same size as the handles. Take the lining out of the basket.

5. For each handle, cut a length of ribbon slightly longer than the sides and base of the handle rectangle and press it in half widthways. Pin, tack and machine stitch the ribbon around the handle of the lining, folding the ribbon neatly at the corners.

6. Cut a length of ribbon to fit around one side of the lining plus 60 cm/24 in. Press in half widthways and pin, tack and machine stitch it along one side of the lining leaving 30 cm/12 in. of ribbon free at each end. Repeat along the other side of the lining. Press and place the lining inside the basket, tying the ribbons with a neat bow at either end.

Door stop

This stylish door stop made from striking floral and spotted fabrics can be moved around as and when it is needed. You could simplify the design by using just one fabric and replacing the fabric handle with wide cotton ribbon.

YOU WILL NEED

25 cm/10 in. patterned fabric
25 cm/10 in. spotted fabric
75-cm/30-in. length of 5-mm/¼-in. ribbon
Thick cardboard
Dried peas
Stuffing
Sewing machine and matching sewing thread

Take 1.5-cm/½-in. seam allowances throughout unless otherwise stated.

1. Cut out two 21 x 15-cm/8¼ x 6-in. and two 18 x 15-cm/7 x 6-in. rectangles of patterned fabric. Cut two 21 x 9-cm/8¼ x 3½-in. and two 18 x 9-cm/7 x 3½-in. rectangles of spotted fabric.

2. With right sides together, pin and machine stitch a spotted rectangle to a patterned rectangle of the same width, until you have four panels. (These will form the sides of the door stop.) Press the seams open.

3. Pin and machine stitch a length of ribbon over the seam on all four panels of fabric.

4. For the top and bottom of the door stop, cut a 21 x 18-cm/8$\frac{1}{4}$ x 7-in. rectangle of each fabric.

5. Cut a 25 x 11-cm/10 x 4$\frac{1}{4}$-in. strip of patterned fabric for the handle. With right sides together, fold the strip in half lengthways and pin and machine stitch along the longest edge. Turn right side out and press. Pin the handle centrally across the fabric for the top of the door stop, turning under the ends. At each end, machine stitch a rectangle about 5.5 cm/2$\frac{1}{4}$ in. long to attach the handle firmly.

6. With right sides together, pin and machine stitch the four side panels together, alternating the sizes of the panels, to form a loop. Press the seams open.

7. With right sides together, pin and machine stitch the top of the door stop to the side piece. Snip the corners. Pin and stitch the bottom piece to the bottom of the sides in the same way, leaving one short side open. Turn right side out and press.

8. Cut two 18 x 15-cm/7 x 6-in. pieces of card and push them inside the fabric box, one at the bottom and one at the top. Half fill the box with stuffing and then pour in dried peas until the box is fairly solid. Hand stitch the open side closed.

Sewing kit

3 hours

With this neat little sewing kit, all your needles, pins, thread and buttons can be kept just where you need them. Made from a bold spotted fabric and lined with felt, it can be adapted to hold all kinds of things, from sewing and knitting accessories to stationery and art equipment, and is easily portable, too.

YOU WILL NEED

50 cm/20 in. red felt
50 cm/20 in. spotted fabric
50 cm/20 in. medium-weight iron-on interfacing
Sewing machine and matching sewing thread
Large press stud
Large button
Sewing items for the kit – embroidery threads, needles, pins, tape measure, buttons, tailor's chalk etc.

Take 1.5-cm/^{1}/$_2$-in. seam allowances throughout unless otherwise stated.

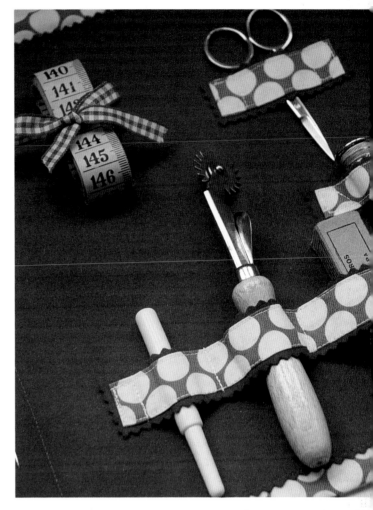

1. Using pinking shears, cut a 42 x 24-cm/16^1/$_2$ x9^1/$_2$-in. rectangle of red felt. Press with a warm iron. Measure 10 cm/4 in. in from each short end and mark with pins to show where the folds will be.

2. Lay the felt on your work surface and arrange the contents of the sewing kit on it, avoiding the fold lines. Cut rectangles of spotted fabric 2 cm/^{3}/$_4$ in. wide and as long as necessary to hold the items in place, adding 3 cm/1^1/$_4$ in. all around each piece. Fold under 1.5 cm/^{1}/$_2$ in. all the way around each rectangle and press. Using pinking shears, cut rectangles of felt 5 mm/^{1}/$_4$ in. bigger all the way round than the fabric rectangles. Machine stitch the fabric rectangles onto the felt pieces.

3. Machine stitch the felt-backed spotted rectangles onto the large felt piece in the required positions. Stitch a 30-cm/12-in. length of ribbon onto the felt to hold the tape measure in place.

4. Cut two 30 x 47.5-cm/12 x 18¾-in. pieces of spotted fabric. Cut two pieces of interfacing the same size. Lay one piece of interfacing on the back of each piece of spotted fabric, rough side down. Place a damp cloth on top and iron with a medium iron to fuse the interfacing to the fabric. Centre the felt panel on the right side of one of the spotted pieces.

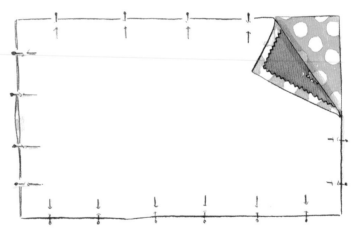

5. Cut two 7-cm/2¾-in. squares of spotted fabric for the tab. With right sides together, pin and stitch around three sides of the fabric. Trim the seam allowance to 5 mm/¼ in., turn right side out and press.

6. Using pinking shears, cut a piece of red felt 5 mm/¼ in. bigger all around than the tab. Centre the tab on the felt and machine stitch in place.

7. With right sides together, pin the front and back of the folder together. Place the tab in the centre of one short side, aligning the raw edge of the spotted fabric with the raw edge of the front. Machine stitch all the way around, leaving an opening of about 8 cm/3 in. in one side. Trim the corners, turn right side out and press.

8. Hand stitch the opening closed. Sew half of the press stud onto the inside of the tab and stitch the other half onto the front of the folder.

9. Stitch the button securely onto the front of the tab. Press the folder and then fill it with the sewing kit.

Fabric-covered storage box

This is a great storage solution for a home office. Make a whole range in different sizes to keep stationery or correspondence close at hand.

YOU WILL NEED

2 co-ordinating fabrics

Thick cardboard

Craft knife, steel rule and cutting mat

Sewing machine and matching sewing thread

Needle and thread

Take 1.5-cm/½-in. seam allowances throughout unless otherwise stated.

WORKING OUT FABRIC QUANTITIES

Decide how tall and wide you want the box to be. Add the measurements for all four sides together, and then add 3 cm/1¼ in. Add 3 cm/1¼ in. to the height of the box. Take the measurement for the box base and add 3 cm/1¼ in. to both the width and the length.

1. To make the handle, cut a 15 x 7.5-cm/6 x 3-in. rectangle of fabric 1. Fold it in half lengthways, pin and machine stitch along the long raw edge. Turn right side out and press. Fold the ends under by 1.5 cm/½ in. and press.

2. Measure 1.5 cm/½ in. from one end of the strip of fabric for the sides of the box and mark with a pin. Measure the width of the box from this mark. Pin on the handle at this point and machine stitch a square at the end. Pin the other end in place and machine stitch in place.

3. With right sides together, pin and machine stitch the short ends of the strip together. Press the seam open.

4. With right sides together, pin and machine stitch the side piece to the base, making sure that the handle is positioned centrally along one short side.

5. Snip the corners and press all the seams open.

6. Cut out the lining from your co-ordinating fabric, using the same measurements as before. With right sides together, pin and machine stitch the short ends of the strip together and press the seam open. With right sides together, pin and machine stitch the side strip to the base, leaving one short side open. Snip the corners and press the seams open.

7. With right sides together, pin and machine stitch the two fabric box shapes together, leaving one short end open. Press the seam open and turn right side out. Form a box shape with the lining on the inside.

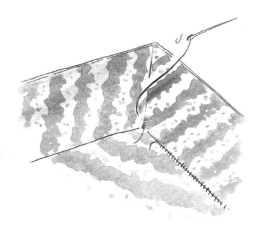

8. Cut out a rectangle of cardboard to fit the base of the box. Insert it into the base of the box through the unstitched opening. Measure and cut two pieces of cardboard for the long sides and two for the short sides. Slot the longer pieces into the sides of the fabric box and the shorter lengths into the ends.

9. Hand stitch the open end closed. Make a few small stitches at each corner through all the layers to hold the lining in place.

Peg board

1 hour

This handy peg board requires very little sewing and provides a stylish and practical place to keep notes and shopping lists. It's also a lovely way of displaying treasured family photos. The pegs that I've used to hold the items in place are smaller than standard wooden clothes pegs and are widely available from craft shops. They are decorated with buttons, but you could also paint them in pretty colours to match the fabric that you've used to cover the board.

YOU WILL NEED

60 x 44 cm/24 x 17½ in. hardboard
Spray adhesive
75 cm/30 in. wadding
75 cm/30 in. striped ticking fabric
25 cm/10 in. floral fabric
Glue gun and general-purpose glue sticks
Miniature clothes pegs (available from craft suppliers)

1. Cut a 60 x 44-cm/24 x 17½-in. piece of wadding. Apply spray adhesive to one side of the hardboard and stick the wadding onto it, pressing it down firmly for a smooth finish.

2. Cut four 5 x 54-cm/2 x 21½-in. lengths of floral fabric. Fold the floral pieces in half lengthways and press. Open out again, fold the raw edges in to the central fold and press. Machine stitch close to the edge.

3. Cut a 70 x 54-cm/28 x 21½-in. piece of ticking fabric. Pin three of the strips across it, making sure they are straight. Position the first strip 20 cm/8 in. from the bottom of the fabric, the second one 14 cm/5½ in. above that, and the third one 14 cm/5½ in. above that. Machine stitch the strips onto the ticking, stitching in from each end for about 5 cm/2 in. Tie a knot in each end of the remaining strips and stitch it onto the ticking 5 cm/2 in. from the top and 17 cm/6¾ in. in from each side.

4. Lay the ticking fabric right side down on your work surface and centre the hardboard on top of it, wadding side down. Fold the surplus fabric over onto the back of the board and use a glue gun to stick it in place, folding the corners in neatly and pulling the fabric taut as you do so.

Fabric-covered picture frame

A covered picture frame can make a treasured family photo even more of a centrepiece. Choose a frame with fairly wide borders and cover with a classic natural linen fabric decorated with ribbon in muted tones, adding pretty ribbon rosettes at the corners for a stylish and unusual look.

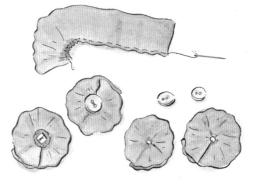

YOU WILL NEED

Ready-made picture frame
Linen
Grosgrain ribbon in two colours
175 cm/90 in. co-ordinating ribbon 22 mm/⅞ in. wide
Needle and thread
8 small decorative buttons
Sewing machine and matching sewing thread
Fast-drying craft glue

1½ hours

1. Cut a piece of linen 8 cm/3¼ in. bigger all around than the frame. Cut a length of the first colour of grosgrain ribbon the same size as each side of the fabric. Pin and machine stitch the ribbons across the width of the fabric 5 cm/2 in. from the top and the bottom. Repeat along the length of the fabric, again placing the ribbons 5 cm/2 in. from the edge of the fabric.

2. Take the second colour of grosgrain ribbon and machine stitch it onto the fabric about 5 mm/¼ in. inside the first ribbon. Turn the ribbon over at each corner neatly.

3. From the centre of the fabric, cut out a rectangle 1.5 cm/½ in. smaller than the inside measurement of the frame. Snip diagonally into each corner to a depth of 1.5 cm/½ in. to create four flaps. Lay the frame on the wrong side of the fabric and glue the flaps of fabric to the wrong side of the frame, holding them in place until firmly stuck. Pull the outer part of the fabric over the back of the frame, fold in the corners neatly and glue in place.

4. Cut eight 20-cm/8-in. lengths of co-ordinating ribbon. Work a line of running stitch along the bottom of each ribbon and pull the thread to gather into a rosette. Finish with a few stitches to hold the ends together and sew a button to the middle of each one. Glue two rosettes onto each corner of the frame.

Floor cushion

1 hour

Make a pile of these comfy floor cushions to sink into with a good book or to provide extra seating when guests come to visit. Use two different fabrics for each cushion and cover the button at the centre of each cushion with a co-ordinating fabric for extra interest. The covers cannot be taken off without removing the buttons, so make sure you use cushion pads that are machine washable so that you can throw the whole thing into the machine for easy cleaning.

YOU WILL NEED

75 cm/30 in. each of two co-ordinating fabrics
Cushion pad 65 cm/25$\frac{1}{2}$ in. square
2 self-cover buttons 3 cm/1$\frac{1}{4}$ in. in diameter
Sewing machine
Needle
Matching sewing thread
Upholstery thread and needle

Take 1.5-cm/$\frac{1}{2}$-in. seam allowances throughout unless otherwise stated.

1. Cut a 68-cm/26$\frac{3}{4}$-in. square of each fabric. Lay one square right side up on your work surface and place the second one right side down on top of it, aligning all edges. Pin and machine stitch all around, leaving a gap of about 30 cm/12 in. in one side. Trim the corners close to the stitching to reduce the bulk.

2. Turn the cover right side out and press. Insert the cushion pad and hand stitch the opening closed, using small stitches. Find the centre point of the cushion cover on both sides and mark with a pin.

3. Following the manufacturer's instructions, cover the buttons with fabric. Thread an upholstery needle and knot the thread. Stitch through the cushion at the central pin and thread on a button. Take the needle back though the cushion and thread a button onto the other side. Pull the thread firmly to pull the buttons into the cushion. Stitch back through the buttons a couple of times and secure with a few stitches.

Roll-up blind

2 hours

YOU WILL NEED

Patterned fabric

Co-ordinating gingham fabric

Sewing machine and matching sewing thread

Dowelling 15 mm/½-in. in diameter

Two metal rings 4 cm/1½-in. in diameter

Length of 5 x 2.5-cm/2 x 1-in. wood

Velcro

Fast-drying craft glue

12-mm/½-in.-ribbon

Take 1.5-cm/½-in. seam allowances throughout unless otherwise stated.

This simple blind, made from a bold floral fabric backed with a co-ordinating gingham check, can be made very quickly. As the blind has to be rolled up manually, it is ideal for rooms where it can be kept raised most of the time. Ribbons tied in pretty bows hold the blind in place when raised. The wooden dowelling in the bottom of the panel ensures that the blind forms a neat roll and does not sag.

1. Cut a piece of patterned fabric and a piece of gingham fabric 3 cm/1¼ in. wider and 7 cm/2¾ in. longer than the finished blind. With right sides together, pin and machine stitch them together along both sides and the bottom. Snip off the corners.

2. Turn right side out and press. Cut a piece of dowelling to fit the width of the panel and push it down inside the blind. Hand stitch just above the dowelling to keep it in place.

3. Make two tabs to hold the metal rings. Cut two 9 x 23-cm/ 3½ x 9-in. rectangles of patterned fabric. With right sides together, fold them in half lengthways and machine stitch 1.5 cm/ ½ in. from the edge. Turn right side out and press, with the seam in the middle of the tab. Thread each tab through a ring and fold in half.

4. Fold the open end of the blind over to the wrong side by 1.5 cm/1/2 in. and again by 4 cm/11/2 in., placing the tabs under the hem 17 cm/7 in. in from each side. Machine stitch along the bottom of the folded panel.

5. Cut a piece of wood the same width as the blind. Cut a piece of patterned fabric 13 cm/5 in. deeper and 4 cm/11/2 in. wider than the wood. Centre the wood on the fabric and glue it in place, folding the corners of the fabric in neatly.

6. Cut a piece of Velcro the same length as the wood and glue one half of it onto the wood. Screw the wood into the window frame.

7. Cut two pieces of ribbon the same length as the blind. Pin and machine stitch the other half of the Velcro to the top of the blind on the wrong side, placing one length of ribbon 17 cm/7 in. in from each side, under the hem.

8. Roll up the blind from the bottom and stick it onto the Velcroed wood. Cut two 25-cm/10-in. lengths of ribbon 12-mm-/1/2-in.- wide ribbon and hand stitch one onto each ring. Bring the ribbon from the back of the blind to the front and tie to the shorter length of ribbon at the ring.

CHAPTER 5

Laundry and bathrooms

Ironing board cover

Even purely functional items such as ironing board covers don't have to be dull! Use a favourite fabric to make a padded cover that is held in place with a drawstring, making it easy to remove and wash. Thick cotton fabrics work best for this project, lined with cotton wadding that will withstand some heat.

1½ hours

YOU WILL NEED

75 cm/30 in. plain white cotton fabric

Pencil or fabric marker

75 cm/30 in. patterned fabric

75 cm/30 in. lightweight cotton wadding

Sewing machine and matching sewing thread

Approx. 2 m/79 in. white ribbon

Take 1.5-cm/½-in. seam allowances throughout unless otherwise stated.

1. Lay the ironing board on the white fabric and draw around it, adding 10 cm/4 in. all around. Cut out. Cut a piece of patterned fabric and a piece of cotton wadding to the same size.

2. Lay the patterned fabric right side up on your work surface. Place the white cotton on top, with the wadding on top of the cotton. Pin and machine stitch through all the layers, leaving an opening of about 15 cm/6 in. at the straight end. Snip the seam allowance off at the corners and trim the seam allowance to 5 mm/¼ in. all the way around.

3. Turn the cover right side out and press. Measure and machine stitch a line 5 cm/2 in. from the edge all the way around.

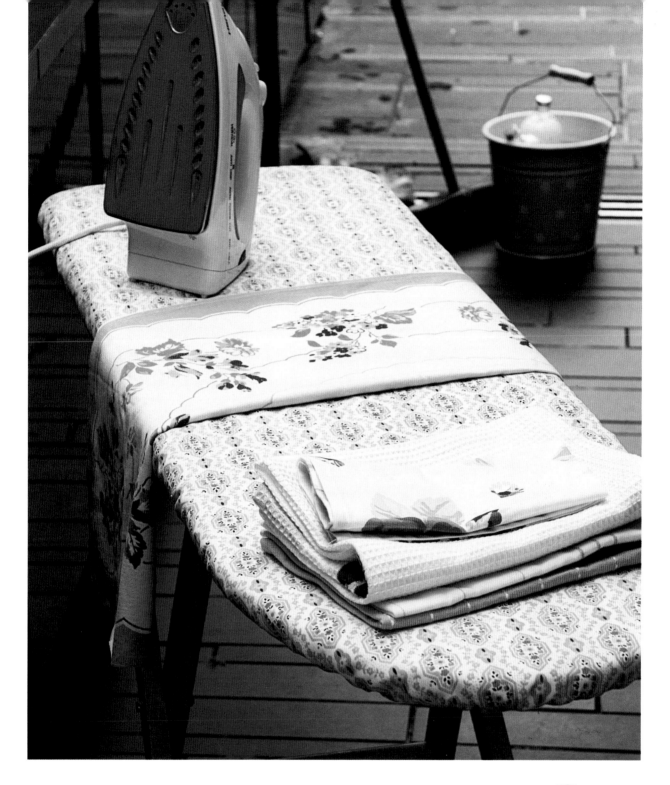

4. Attach a safety pin to the end of the ribbon and thread it through the channel all the way around the cover. Pull the ribbon to gather the cover over the ironing board and secure with a bow.

Towelling bath mat

2 hours

YOU WILL NEED

50 cm/20 in. cream towelling fabric
1 m/40 in. patterned fabric
25 cm/10 in. border fabric
2 m/78½ in. ricrac braid
Sewing machine
Matching sewing thread

Take 1.5-cm/½-in. seam allowances throughout unless otherwise stated.

The mitred corners on this bath mat give a smart, professional finish but they are surprisingly easy to achieve. The patterned fabric that I used, with its colourful bathroom motifs, is absolutely perfect, but of course you could use any fabric you wish – although it is worth avoiding stripes and checks, which are harder to match up at the corners. Make sure you choose a good-quality, thick towelling for the centre of the mat, to make it super soft on your feet.

1. From both the patterned fabric and the border fabric, cut two 78 x 14-cm/30¾ x 5½-in. strips and two 67 x 14-cm/26⅜ x 5½-in. strips. With right sides together, pin and machine stitch each border piece to a patterned piece of the same length. Press the seams open.

2. Measure 15.5 cm/6¼ in. in from the end of the border fabric and make a pencil mark. Using a ruler, draw a diagonal line from this mark to the edge of the patterned fabric. Cut along the line. Repeat at each end of the four strips of fabric.

3. With right sides together, machine stitch one long and one short border piece together along the mitred edge. Repeat with the other two border pieces, then join them together to create a frame shape. Press the seams open.

4. Cut a 34 x 47.5-cm/13$\frac{1}{2}$ x 18$\frac{5}{8}$-in. piece of towelling fabric. With right sides together, pin and stitch the towelling to the inside edge of the border all the way around.

5. Cut a 71 x 59-cm/28 x 23$\frac{1}{4}$-in. piece of patterned fabric for the back of the mat. With right sides together, pin and machine stitch the front and back pieces together, leaving an opening of about 15 cm/6 in. in one side. Trim the corners and turn right side out.

6. Hand stitch the opening closed.

7. Pin the ricrac braid 1.5 cm/$\frac{1}{2}$ in. from the small border all the way around the mat, folding it at the corners for a neat finish, and machine stitch it in place.

Towel with fabric border

Transform plain towels with an attractively patterned fabric border. The neat little hanging loop is a professional-looking finishing touch and means that they can be displayed on a peg rail or door hook when not in use, adding a splash of colour and pattern to your bathroom. Make a set of bath and hand towels for a personal and unique gift, choosing fabrics in colours that tone in with the recipient's bathroom.

3 hours

1. Cut a 71 x 24-cm/28 x 9½-in. piece of patterned fabric, a 71 x 27-cm/28 x 10½-in. piece of gingham fabric and a 71 x 6-cm/28 x 2¼-in. piece of gingham fabric. With right sides together, pin and machine stitch one gingham piece along each long edge of the patterned fabric. Press the seams open.

2. To make the fabric hanging loop, cut a 19 x 5-cm/7½ x 2-in. piece of patterned fabric. With wrong sides together, fold in half lengthways and press. Open out and fold both long edges in to the central fold. Press. Fold in half again, aligning the folded edges. Pin, then machine stitch close to the edge. Press.

3. Lay the towel on your work surface, with the fabric border right side down on top of it 22.5 cm/8½ in. from one short edge of the towel. Place the fabric loop under this about 3 cm/1¼ in. on either side of the middle of the towel (widthways), with the two raw ends sticking out. Pin, tack and machine stitch in place.

4. Fold the fabric border down over the towel and up over itself, with right sides together. Fold over 1.5 cm/½ in. along the top edge of the border and line it up with the border stitched to the towel. Machine stitch along both sides of the towel and trim the seams. Turn right side out, tucking in the end of the towel. Slipstitch the remaining border edge in place.

Drawstring laundry bag

Practical and stylish, this pretty laundry bag looks great in both the bathroom or bedroom, as well as providing a roomy and functional place to store worn clothes that are awaiting washing. The neat fabric loop means that it can be hung on the back of a door, while the drawstring close makes for easy, everyday use.

3 hours

YOU WILL NEED

50 cm/20 in. patterned fabric
1 m/40 in. spotty fabric
1 m/40 in. co-ordinating fabric for the lining
1 m/40 in. medium-weight iron-on interfacing
Sewing machine
Matching sewing thread
Paper for pattern

Take 1.5-cm/½-in. seam allowances throughout unless otherwise stated.

1. Cut a 102 x 25-cm/40 x 10-in. rectangle of patterned fabric and two 102 x 20-cm/40 x 8-in. rectangles of spotty fabric. Lay the patterned piece right side up on your work surface, with one of the spotty pieces right side down on top, aligning along one long raw edge. Pin, tack and machine stitch together.

2. Pin, tack and machine stitch the other spotty piece along the other raw edge. Open out both seams and press.

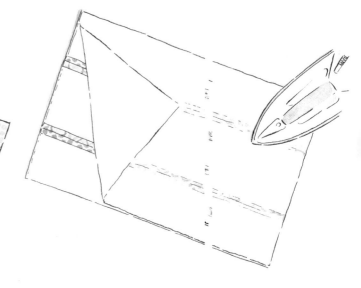

3. Cut a 102 x 65-cm/40 x 25½-in. piece of interfacing. Lay the interfacing on the wrong side of the fabric panel, with the rough side down. Place a damp cloth on top and iron with a medium iron to fuse the interfacing to the fabric.

4. With right sides together, pin, tack and machine stitch the side edges together, leaving a 2-cm/¾-in. opening 9.5 cm/3¾ in. from the top edge.

5. Draw a circle 33.5 cm/13 in. in diameter on paper and cut out to make a template for the base of the bag. Pin the template to the spotty fabric, draw around it and cut out. Cut a piece of interfacing the same size and iron to the reverse of the spotty fabric, as before. With right sides together, pin, tack and machine stitch the base to the sides of the bag. Make small snips all the way around the seam allowance.

6. Cut a 102 x 48.5-cm/40 x 19-in. rectangle of fabric for the lining. Pin, tack and machine stitch along the short sides to form a tube. Press the seam open. Cut a circle of fabric and a circle of interfacing, as for the base of the bag, and iron together as before. Pin, tack and machine stitch the base onto the lining, again making small snips around the seam allowance.

7. With wrong sides together, place the lining inside the bag. Fold over and press 1.5 cm/½ in. and then another 5 cm/2 in. around the top of the bag. Machine stitch as close as possible to the edge, and then work another line of stitching 2 cm/¾ in. below that, to form a channel.

8. Cut a 140 x 5-cm/55 x 2-in. strip of fabric. Fold in half lengthways. Open out, fold in 1 cm/$^3/_8$ in. along each long side, and press. Fold the strip in half again and stitch along it to make the drawstring.

9. Thread the drawstring through the channel at the top of the bag and tie with a knot. Cut a 23 x 5-cm/9 x 2-in. piece of fabric. Fold in half, right sides together, and machine stitch along the two long edges. Turn right side out and turn the raw ends under by 1.5 cm/$^1/_2$ in. Stitch onto the bag to form a loop, stitching it onto the bag above and below the drawstring channel.

Peg bag

This charming bag is the perfect place to store wooden clothes pegs and will brighten up any wash day. I used a vintage-style floral fabric topped off with a co-ordinating ribbon and ricrac braid, with a bright gingham lining just visible around the opening. A child's wooden hanger is the perfect size to use inside the bag, so that you can hang it on a hook in the kitchen or utility room when not in use or on the washing line when you are pegging out the laundry.

YOU WILL NEED

Templates on page 166

Tracing paper and pencil

Pattern paper

50 cm/20 in. floral fabric

50 cm/20 in. gingham fabric

50 cm/20 in. pink grosgrain ribbon, 1 cm/3⁄8 in. wide

50 cm/20 in. blue ricrac braid

Sewing machine and matching sewing threads

Take 1.5-cm/1⁄2-in. seam allowances throughout unless otherwise stated.

1. Enlarge the templates on page 166 by 195% and make paper patterns (see page 162). Cut one back piece and one top and one bottom front piece from floral fabric. Repeat using the gingham fabric. Right sides together, pin and then machine stitch the floral and gingham top pieces together along the curve. Trim the seam allowance, turn right side out and press.

2. Lay the gingham bottom front piece right side up on your work surface. Place the top front piece right side up on top of it and the floral bottom front piece wrong side up on top of that. Machine stitch along the top edge, stitching through all layers.

3. Turn right side out and press. Pin a length of blue ricrac braid across the bag about 1.5 cm/1⁄2 in. from the top of the base, with a length of pink grosgrain ribbon about 1 cm/3⁄8 in. below that, and machine stitch in place.

4. Lay the front of the bag right side up on your work surface, with the floral back piece right side down on top of it. Place the gingham back piece right side up on top. Machine stitch all around the edge, leaving a gap of about 2 cm/¾ in. in the centre top. Turn right side out. Insert the coat hanger, and stitch a grosgrain ribbon bow below the hook.

Ribbon and button lavender bag

1½ hours

Lavender has been used for centuries to freshen and scent linens, and these lovely bags can easily be slipped into drawers and linen cupboards to add a gentle fragrance. They are an effective way of using up small scraps of fabric and are finished beautifully with oddments of ribbon, braid and pretty little vintage buttons.

YOU WILL NEED

25 cm/10 in. each of two co-ordinating fabrics

25 cm/10 in. each of two co-ordinating ribbons

25 cm/10 in. ricrac braid

Sewing machine

Needle and matching sewing thread

Dried lavender

Small funnel

Small buttons

Take ½-in./1.5-cm seam allowances throughout unless otherwise stated.

1. Cut two 18 x 15-cm/7 x 6-in. rectangles of your main fabric and two 18 x 11-cm/7 x 4¼-in. rectangles of a co-ordinating fabric. With right sides together, pin and machine stitch one of each size of rectangle together. Press the seams open.

2. Cut two 19-cm/7½-in. lengths of co-ordinating ribbons. Pin and machine stitch one ribbon along the seam on one piece of fabric, to hide the join, and the other about 5 mm/¼ in. from the first, on the smaller section of fabric. Press.

3. Measure and cut a 69-cm/27-in. length of ricrac braid. Lay the ribbon-trimmed piece of fabric right side up on your work surface. Pin and tack the ricrac braid all the way around the edge of the fabric, easing the braid at the corners so that the centre of the ricrac is exactly in line with the seam allowance.

4. With right sides together, lay the second piece of fabric on top of the first. Pin, tack and machine stitch all the way around the pieces, leaving a gap of about 5 cm/2 in. at one end. Trim the corners and trim the seams to 1 cm/³⁄₈ in.

5. Turn the bag the right side out and gently pull the corners out for a neat finish. Press. Fill the bag with dried lavender using a small funnel. Alternatively, stuff the bag with cotton stuffing and add a little dried lavender. Hand stitch the opening closed, turning in the seam allowance. Stitch buttons onto the ribbon for extra decoration.

Padded coat hanger

Padded hangers look much prettier than plain wooden ones and are much kinder to your clothes. This hanger is made from scraps of fabric and takes no time at all to make. The flower is made from simple petal shapes hand stitched together and finishes the hanger off beautifully. Ideal as a gift, you could throw in some dried lavender before stitching the cover on to fragrance it, too.

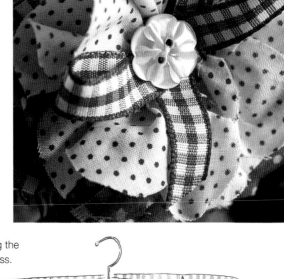

1 hour

1. Cover the coat hanger with wadding, stitching the wadding securely in place, and trim off any excess. Enlarge the template on page 168 by 236% (see page 162). Trace onto the main fabric and cut out. Turn under and press 1 cm/⅜ in. to the wrong side all around. Lay the padded coat hanger on the top half of the fabric and fold up the bottom half to cover the hanger.

2. Starting from the centre and working outwards on each side, using double thread, work a row of large running stitches (see page 163) along the top of the hanger, gathering the fabric slightly as you go and securing it at the end.

3. Using the template on page 168, cut four large flower shapes from gingham fabric. Work a small circle of running stitches in the centre of each flower, then pull the thread to gather the fabric. Stitch the four shapes together at their gathered points to form one complete flower.

4. Repeat with two spotty fabrics, making the final layer smaller. Stitch all three flowers together. Stitch a red-and-white gingham ribbon bow to the centre of the flower with a button.

Half curtain

A curtain that covers half a window is a great way of screening the view while still letting in light. This charming panel is made from strips of fabric sewn together, and can easily be tied in place and taken down when not needed, using ribbon ties at the corners.

YOU WILL NEED

3 co-ordinating fabrics

Lining fabric

2 co-ordinating 10-mm/³⁄₈-in. ribbons twice the length of the finished curtain plus 10 cm/4 in.

2 m/79 in. length of 15-mm/⁵⁄₈-in. ribbon for ties

Sewing machine

Needle and thread

2 hooks

Take 1.5-cm/½-in. seam allowances throughout unless otherwise stated.

WORKING OUT FABRIC QUANTITIES

To work out the width of each fabric strip, measure the width of the window, divide by five and add 3 cm/1¼ in. To work out the length of each strip, measure half the depth of the window and add 8 cm/3 in.

1. Cut two strips of two of the fabrics and one strip of the third fabric to the required size (see left). With right sides together, pin and machine stitch the strips together, with the single strip in the centre and one strip of each other fabric on either side.

2. Press the seams open. On the right side of the fabric, lay one piece of ribbon over each seam. Pin, tack and machine stitch the ribbons in place. Trim the ends to the same length as the fabric. Press.

3. Cut a piece of lining the same size as the front panel. Along each side of both the lining and the front panel, turn over 2 cm/ ³⁄₄ in. to the wrong side. Press. Along the bottom of both the lining and the front panel, turn under 1 cm/³⁄₈ in. and then another 4 cm/ 1½ in. to the wrong side. Machine stitch in place. With wrong sides together and aligning the top raw edges, lay the lining on the front panel. Hand stitch the lining to the front down both sides.

4. Turn the top edge of both the front panel and the lining over to the back of the curtain by 1 cm/³⁄₈ in. and then by another 2 cm/ ³⁄₄ in. and pin. Cut two 50-cm/19-in. lengths of 15-mm/⁵⁄₈-in. ribbon and fold in half. Insert the fold of each ribbon under the pinned hem at either end of the top of the curtain. Machine stitch in place and then fold the ribbon back and work a few hand stitches so that ribbon is fixed to the top of curtain.

Outside spaces

Mattress cushion for garden bench

This generously padded cushion transforms a hard garden chair or bench into a comfy corner in which to relax. The pretty felt tufts add a decorative touch and also hold all the layers of the cushion together.

YOU WILL NEED

1 m/40 in. striped fabric
125 cm/49 in. thick wadding
Sewing machine and matching sewing thread
25 cm/10 in. felt in two colours
Embroidery thread
Long needle

Take 1.5-cm/½-in. seam allowances throughout unless otherwise stated.

ADJUSTING THE SIZES TO FIT YOUR BENCH

The instructions given here are for a cushion that is 50 cm/20 in. square. If you need to adjust the measurements to fit your bench, remember to add 3 cm/1¼ in. to the squares that you cut in Step 1 to allow for the seams. Similarly, the side strip needs to be 3 cm/1¼ in. longer than the sum of the four sides – although the depth will remain the same.

1. Cut two 53-cm/21-in. squares of striped fabric.

2. Cut two strips of fabric 14 cm/5½ in. long by the width of the fabric. Cut off the selvedges. With right sides together, machine stitch the two strips together. Press the seam open. Cut the strip to 203 cm/80 in. long.

3. To make the handle, cut a 24 x 9-cm/9 x 3½-in. strip of fabric. Fold in half lengthways, with right sides together, and machine stitch down the long raw edge. Turn right side out and press so that the seam runs down the centre. Turn the ends under to the wrong side by 1.5 cm/½ in. and press.

4. Pin the handle onto the long fabric strip with one end 15.5 cm/6¹⁄₂ in. from one end and the other end 19 cm/7¹⁄₂ in. from that. Machine stitch a square around each end of the strip and then a cross from corner to corner of the stitched squares.

5. With right sides together, pin and machine stitch the short ends of the long strip together. Press the seam open. With right sides together, pin and machine stitch the side panel to one of the squares, placing the seam of the side panel at a corner. Snip the corners of the square and press.

6. Pin and stitch the other side of the side panel to the remaining square, leaving an opening of about 20 cm/8 in. in one side, and turn right side out. Cut four 50-cm/20-in. squares of wadding. Push them through the opening, making sure that the corners of the wadding are pushed right into the corners of the cover. Hand stitch the opening closed.

7. Using pinking shears, cut four 6-cm/2$\frac{1}{2}$-in. circles from one colour of felt and four 4-cm/1$\frac{1}{2}$-in. circles from the second colour of felt.

8. At each corner, place a pin 16 cm/6 in. in from each side to mark the positions for the felt circles. Thread a long needle with embroidery thread and tie a knot about 4 cm/1$\frac{1}{2}$ in. from the end. Thread the needle through the centre of a small felt circle and then through a larger felt circle and push the needle through the cushion at the marked place. Pull the thread through the cushion.

9. Stitch back up from the back of the cushion to the front through the felt circles. Repeat to secure. Pull the thread to gather the cushion and tie a knot to secure it. Trim the ends of the thread to about 3 cm/1$\frac{1}{4}$ in. Repeat at the other corners.

1. First, make a paper pattern for your chair seat, adding 1.5 cm/½ in. all around for the seam allowances. Fold the floral fabric in half to form two layers, and lay the paper pattern on top. Pin the pattern in place and cut out. Remove the pins and paper pattern.

4 hours

Garden chair cushion with frill

These pretty seat cushions add a touch of comfort to simple garden chairs and bring a delightfully summery feel to any patio or garden. A vintage-style floral fabric is used for the main seat cover, trimmed with a dainty frill made from a co-ordinating spotty fabric. For an extra decorative touch a simple slip cover, which could easily be padded for more comfort, sits snugly on the back rest.

2. For the frill, cut a 10.5 x 200-cm/4 x 78½-in. length of spotted fabric. (Join pieces together if necessary to make the required length and press open the seams.) Fold over 1 cm/⅜ in. and then 1.5 cm/½ in. along one long edge. Pin and machine stitch. Press. Fold both short ends of the strip over by 1 cm/⅜ in. and again by 1.5 cm/½ in. Pin and machine stitch.

YOU WILL NEED

Pattern paper
50 cm/20 in. main floral fabric
50 cm/20 in. spotty fabric
25-cm/10-in. zip
Sewing machine
Needle and matching sewing thread
Foam cushion pad to fit chair

Take 1.5-cm/½-in. seam allowances throughout unless otherwise stated.

3. Take a needle and thread and work a loose running stitch along the length of the strip, about 1 cm/⅜ in. in from the raw edge. Gently pull the thread to gather the fabric, making sure that the gathers are even. The finished frill should be the same length as the sides and front edge of your garden seat. Finish with a few small stitches.

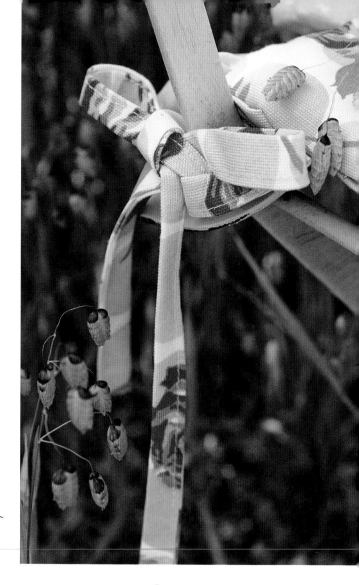

4. Lay one piece of floral fabric right side up on your work surface. With right sides together, aligning the raw edges, pin the frill around the sides and front edge, and tack in place.

5. To make the ties, cut four 6 x 45-cm/2¼ x 17¼-in. pieces of floral fabric. Lay one piece wrong side up on your work surface. Fold over one short end and both long sides by 1.5 cm/½ in. Press. Fold the strip in half widthways, aligning the edges. Pin and machine stitch along the folded-over short end and along the length, stitching as close to the edge as possible. Repeat with the other three pieces of fabric.

6. Lay the cushion piece with the frill right side up on your work surface. Aligning the raw edges, pin and tack two pairs of ties along the back edge of the cushion piece, placing each pair about 5 cm/2 in. from one side edge.

7. With right sides together, pin the two cushion pieces together along the back edge, sandwiching the frill in between. Mark the centre 25 cm/10 in. along the back edge with pins. Machine stitch up to the pins on either side. Tack the centre 25 cm/10 in. Press open the seam. Pin and tack the zip into the tacked part of the seam. Machine stitch in place, using a zipper foot on your machine. Remove the tacking stitches. Open the zip.

8. Pin and stitch the three open sides of the cushion cover. Make small snips at the corners. Turn the cover right side out and press. Insert the cushion pad and close the zip.

9. To make the back rest cover, measure and cut rectangles of floral fabric 2.5 cm/1 in. bigger all around than the back rest of your chair. With right sides together, pin and stitch the fabric pieces together along three sides. Trim the corners. On the remaining raw edge, turn under a double 1-cm/3/8-in. hem. Pin and machine stitch in place. Press.

VARIATION

Replace the frill with a length of ricrac braid.

2 m/79 in. striped fabric

150 cm/60 in. cotton tape

Sewing machine and matching
sewing thread

Template on page 169

Tracing paper, pencil and paper
for pattern

Tailor's chalk

6 large buttons

Two 15-mm/⅝-in. metal eyelets

Hammer to fix the eyelets

Two lengths of 2-cm/¾-in.
wooden dowelling

Two wooden finials

Approx. 3 m/3 yd cord

Pinking shears

Bradawl

Take 1.5-cm/½-in. seam
allowances throughout unless
otherwise stated.

Awning

Create shade and shelter with this simple garden awning. Use heavyweight cotton or canvas and metal eyelets to make an instant garden canopy that is easy to put up and is very transportable. The awning can be tied to any sturdy structure such as fencing or trees; you could even attach it to the side of your house to create a shady patio area by fitting hooks to the wall.

1. Turn over and pin 1 cm/⅜ in. and then another 1.5 cm/½ in. on all sides of the striped fabric. Cut two 75-cm/30-in. lengths of cotton tape, fold in half and machine stitch at two of the corners.

2. At the opposite end to the tapes, fold over 24 cm/9½ in. to the wrong side. Enlarge the template on page 169 by 115%, trace onto paper to make a pattern and cut out. Lay the pattern on the folded-over section and draw around it with tailor's chalk, moving it along each time until there are six triangles to form a line of 'bunting'.

3. Machine stitch along the chalk lines. Cut around the triangles with pinking shears about 5 mm/¼ in. from the stitched line.

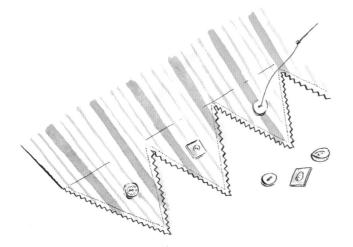

4. Hand stitch a button onto each triangle.

5. Following the manufacturer's instructions, fix an eyelet at each side of the bunting.

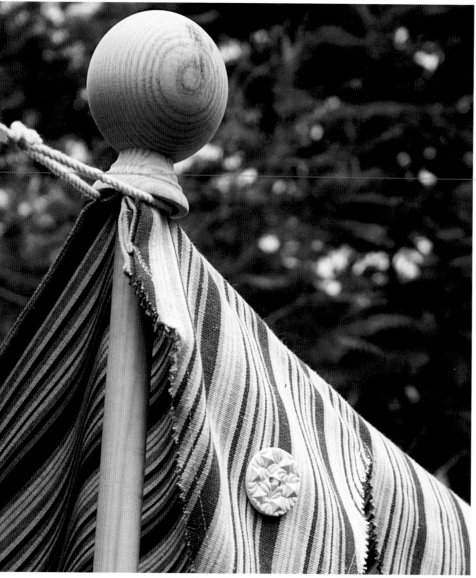

6. Cut the dowelling to the required length. Using a bradawl, make a hole in one end of each piece of dowelling.

7. Place a piece of dowelling on the underside of an eyelet, and screw a finial into it securely.

8. Tie the tape onto hooks screwed into a wall or to the branches of a tree. Push the ends of the dowelling into the ground, pulling the awning taut. Loop cord around the bottom of the finials, pull taut and fasten to the ground with tent pegs.

YOU WILL NEED

Templates on page 170

Tracing paper, pencil and paper
for patterns

6 m/237 in. patterned fabric

6 m/237 in. fabric for lining

175 cm/69 in. ribbon 2 cm/³⁄₄ in. wide

Sewing machine and matching sewing
thread

Needle and thread

4 x 2-m/78-in. lengths of 15-mm/¹⁄₂-in.
dowelling

Take 1.5-cm/¹⁄₂-in. seam allowances
throughout unless otherwise stated.

Children's play tent

6 hours

Children will love this play tent! Made in a traditional tepee shape, it requires moderate sewing skill and takes slightly longer to make than many of the other projects in this book – but don't be put off! It really is worth the effort and is sturdy enough to last for many years, guaranteeing hours and hours of fun for all those who are lucky enough to play in it.

1. Draw pattern templates following the dimensions given on the templates on page 170 and cut out. Pin the patterns to your chosen fabric and cut three pieces of fabric for the sides of the text and two for the front. With right sides together, pin and machine stitch the three side pieces together. Press the seams open. With right sides together, following the diagram, pin and machine stitch one front piece to each side. Press the seams open.

2. Repeat Step 1 using the lining fabric.

3. With right sides together, pin and machine stitch the two front panels together from the top down for a distance of about 90 cm/36 in. Press the seam open. Repeat on the lining fabric.

4. With right sides together, pin the lining to the main fabric around the bottom edge, matching the seams of both fabrics. Machine stitch in place, leaving a gap of 2.5 cm/1 in. at either side of each seam and stitching around the opening for the door. Snip the seam at the top of the door opening and turn the tent right side out.

5. On the main fabric, press under 1.5 cm/½ in. around the top of the tent and machine stitch in place. Repeat with the lining fabric. Pin, tack and machine stitch a line from the bottom to the top of the tent 2.5 cm/1 in. from each seam to form four corner channels.

6. Hand stitch around the top of the tent between the channels to join the main fabric and lining fabrics together.

7. Cut a 50-cm/20-in. length of ribbon. Measure halfway along it and machine stitch it onto the tent 5 cm/2 in. from the top, in the centre of the back panel of the tent.

8. Cut four 30-cm/12-in. lengths of ribbon. Machine stitch one ribbon to the bottom corner of each door opening, folding under 1.5 cm/¹⁄₂ in. at the end. Stitch the remaining two ribbons onto the seam between the front and side panels 55 cm/21¹⁄₂ in. from the bottom of the tent, taking care not to stitch through the channel.

9. Push the dowelling poles up through the corner channels and push the bottom ends of the poles into the ground slightly so that the side panels are pulled flat. (You may need an extra pair of hands for this!) Gather up the top of the tent around the poles and tie the ribbon several times around it, tying with a bow to secure.

Picnic blanket

3 hours

Bright, cheerful fabrics in various tones of sunshine yellow make this the perfect blanket for a summer picnic. Make sure that all the fabrics you choose are machine washable, so that the blanket is easy to clean, and use a heavy cotton fabric for the backing to give it some weight.

YOU WILL NEED

150 cm/60 in. patterned fabric
50 cm/20 in. each of two spotted fabrics
2 m/80 in. heavyweight gingham fabric for backing
6.5 m/256 in. grosgrain ribbon 22 mm/⅞ in. wide
Sewing machine and matching sewing thread
Needle and thread

Take 1.5-cm/½-in. seam allowances throughout unless otherwise stated.

1. From each spotted fabric, cut eighteen 15-cm/5¾-in. squares. To speed things up, you can make a paper pattern the right size, then fold the fabric several times, pin the pattern on top, and cut through several layers at once.

2. Alternating the fabrics, pin and machine stitch the squares together into two strips of eight squares and two strips of ten.

3. Cut a 99-cm/39-in. square of patterned fabric. With right sides together, pin and machine stitch the two eight-square strips to opposite sides of the large square. Press the seams open.

4. With right sides together, pin and machine stitch the longer strips to the two remaining sides of the square, making sure that each corner square is next to a different spotted fabric. Press the seams open.

5. Cut a 123-cm/48½-in. square of gingham fabric for the back of the blanket. With right sides together, pin and machine stitch the front and back of the blanket together, leaving an opening of about 20 cm/8 in. along one side. Trim the corners and turn right side out.

6. Press the blanket and hand stitch the opening closed.

7. Lay the blanket on your work surface and pin, tack and machine stitch grosgrain ribbon all the way round the seam between the border and the central square, turning the ribbon over at each corner for a neat finish.

8. Cut four 22-cm/9-in. lengths of grosgrain ribbon and form each one into a loop. Stitch the ends together. Cut four 6-cm/2½-in. pieces of ribbon and wrap one around the middle of each ribbon loop to form four bows, securing each one with a few stitches at the back. Stitch one bow onto each corner over the stitched ribbon.

Pet basket

This cute animal basket makes the perfect bed for your pet. The size given here is suitable for a cat or small dog, but it can easily be increased in size for larger dogs. The toy, which is made from scraps of fabric, will keep your pet company while the cord that fastens it to the basket will ensure that it never strays too far away. You could even fill the toy with catnip to make the perfect playmate for your feline friend.

YOU WILL NEED

1 m/40 in. patterned fabric
Paper for pattern
Pencil and string
Drawing pin
Templates on page 171
Sewing machine and matching sewing thread
Scraps of fabric for the toy
Stuffing
2 small buttons
20-cm/8-in. length of ribbon for bow
Thick washable wadding

Take 1.5-cm/½-in. seam allowances throughout unless otherwise stated.

1. Fold a piece of paper in half and then into quarters. Tie a piece of string around a pencil. Pin the string to the folded corner of the paper, leaving a 24-cm/9½-in. length of string. Draw a quarter circle on the paper and cut out. This will be the paper pattern for the base of the basket. Lay the paper pattern on a double thickness of patterned fabric and cut out.

2. Enlarge the side-panel template on page 171 by 400%, trace onto paper and cut out. Pin the paper pattern onto your chosen fabric and cut out. With right sides together, pin and machine stitch the ends together and press open the seam.

3. With right sides together, pin and stitch the side panel onto one of the base circles. Make small snips all the way around the seam allowance and press the seam open.

4. To make the toy, cut a 9 x 13-cm/3$\frac{1}{2}$ x 5-in. piece of plain fabric, a 5 x 13-cm/2 x 5-in. strip of patterned fabric and a 6 x 13-cm/2$\frac{1}{4}$ x 5-in. strip of patterned fabric. With right sides together, pin and machine stitch the strips together. Trace the toy template on page 171 onto paper and cut out. Pin the pattern onto the fabric panel and cut out. Then pin the paper pattern onto plain fabric and cut out. Cut four arms from patterned fabric.

5. With right sides together, stitch two arm pieces together, leaving the straight side open. Fill with stuffing. Repeat with the remaining two arm pieces. Pin the two pieces for the toy together with the arms in between, aligning the raw edges. Stitch all around, leaving a 4-cm/1$\frac{1}{2}$-in. gap in one side. Turn right side out and fill with stuffing. Stitch the opening closed and sew on buttons for eyes and a bow at the neck.

6. Cut a 78 x 6-cm/31 x 2$\frac{1}{2}$-in. strip of patterned fabric. Fold it in half lengthways, wrong sides together, and then fold the raw edges in to the centre crease. Machine stitch along the length, stitching as close to the edge as possible.

7. Using the template on page 171, cut out the inner side panel. With right sides together, pin and machine stitch the ends together and press open the seam. Pin and machine stitch the inner side panel onto the remaining base circle, inserting one end of the fabric ribbon into the seam, and leaving an opening of about 20 cm/8 in. Make small snips all the way around the seam allowance. Press.

8. With right sides together, pin and machine stitch the outer side panel to the inner panel. Make small snips around the curved sections and turn right side out. Press.

9. Using the paper patterns that you cut earlier, cut out wadding pieces and insert them through the opening into the base and around the sides to form a basket shape. Hand stitch the opening closed and sew the toy onto the end of the fabric ribbon. Make a few stitches around the inside base of the basket through all the layers to hold the wadding in place.

Techniques and templates

Techniques

The sewing techniques used in this book are all very simple, allowing you to create stylish soft furnishings and accessories for your home quickly and easily. You need only minimal equipment – sharp scissors for cutting fabric and thread, a selection of hand-sewing needles, tailor's chalk, some tracing paper, a pencil or fabric marker pen and a basic sewing machine.

USING TEMPLATES AND PATTERNS

Several of the projects in this book require you to make a template or pattern that you can draw around to cut out a corresponding fabric shape.

ENLARGING MOTIFS TO THE REQUIRED SIZE

Although books and patterns often give motifs at actual size, it is useful to know how to enlarge them.

First, decide how big you want the motif to be on the finished garment. Let's say, for example, that you want a particular shape to be 50 cm/20 in. tall.

Then measure the template that you are working from. Let's imagine that the template is smaller than the size you require – say, 25 cm/10 in. tall.

Take the size that you want the motif to be (50 cm/20 in.) and divide it by the actual size of the template (25 cm/10 in.). Multiply that figure by 100 and you get 200 – so you need to enlarge the motif on a photocopier to 200%.

1. Using a thick black pencil, trace the motif onto tracing paper.

REDUCING MOTIFS TO THE REQUIRED SIZE

If you want a motif on the finished piece to be smaller than the template, the process is exactly the same. For example, if the template is 25 cm/10 in. tall and you want the motif to be 20 cm/8 in. tall, divide 20 cm/8 in. by the actual size of the template (25 cm/10 in.) and multiply by 100, which gives you a figure of 80. So the figure that you need to key in on the photocopier is 80%.

MAKING A TEMPLATE

To make a template for a fabric shape, first enlarge (or reduce) your chosen motif to the size you want.
1. Using a thick black pencil, trace the motif onto tracing paper.

2. Turn the tracing paper over, place it on card, and scribble over your drawn lines to transfer them to the card.

3. Finally, cut out the card shape using scissors or a craft knife on a cutting mat. You can now place the card template on your chosen fabric and draw around it with tailor's chalk or a fabric marker pencil to transfer the shape to the fabric.

HAND STITCHES

These are the most common hand stitches used for joining (either temporarily or permanently) two pieces of fabric together.

TACKING STITCH

Tacking stitch is used to temporarily hold pieces of fabric in place until they have been sewn together permanently. Tacking stitches are removed once the permanent stitching is complete. It's a good idea to use a contrasting colour of thread, so that you can see it easily.

Knot the thread and work a long running stitch (see below) through all layers of fabric.

RUNNING STITCH

Running stitch is probably the simplest hand stitch of all. It is often used to gather a strip of fabric into a frill.

Work from right to left.

Bring the needle up at (a) on the front of the fabric. Take it down again at (b) and up again at (c). Repeat as required.

Tacking stitch

Running stitch

Slipstitch

SLIPSTITCH

This stitch is almost invisible and is an easy method of hemming. It is also used to close openings – for example, when you've left one side of a cushion cover open for turning right side out.

Work from right to left.

Slide the needle between the two pieces of fabric, bringing it out on the edge of the top fabric so that the knot in the thread is hidden between the two layers. Pick up one or two threads from the base fabric, then bring the needle up a short distance along, on the edge of the top fabric, and pull through. Repeat as required.

along, on the edge of the top fabric, and pull through. Repeat
as required.

FASTENINGS

Buttons and zips are the most common fastenings. Modern
sewing machines take the hard work out of making buttonholes
and inserting zips.

MACHINE-STITCHED BUTTONHOLES

Different sewing
machines tend to use
slightly different methods for
stitching buttonholes, so follow the
manufacturer's instructions for your particular machine.

1. Mark the size of the required buttonhole on the fabric with
tailor's chalk or similar. Machine stitch a tight line of zigzag
stitches along each side of the marked line, with a block
of stitches at either end. Most sewing machines
have a special buttonhole foot, which
enables you to do this.

2. Using small, sharp scissors or a seam ripper, cut a slit between the lines of zigzag stitches.

1. With right sides together, pin the two fabric pieces together along the seam allowance. Measure the length of the zip and mark a space centrally on the fabric to this measurement. Stitch from each end of the fabric to the mark for the opening. Tack the open section of the fabric and press the seam open.

2. Lay the closed zip right side down along the tacked area on the wrong side of the fabric and tack in place. Using the zipper foot on your machine, topstitch the zip in place on the right side of the fabric evenly down both sides and across both ends. Remove the tacking stitches and open the zip.

Templates

Add a 1.5-cm/½-in. seam allowance all around each piece
when cutting out.

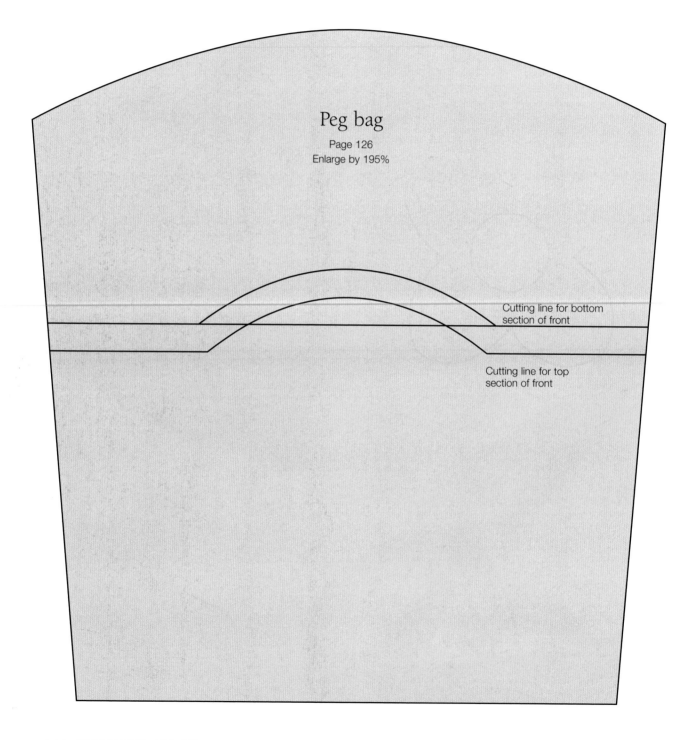

Peg bag

Page 126
Enlarge by 195%

Cutting line for bottom
section of front

Cutting line for top
section of front

Curtain tieback

Page 26
Enlarge by 360%

Tea cosy

Page 34
Enlarge by 203%

Padded coat hanger

Page 130
Enlarge by 236%

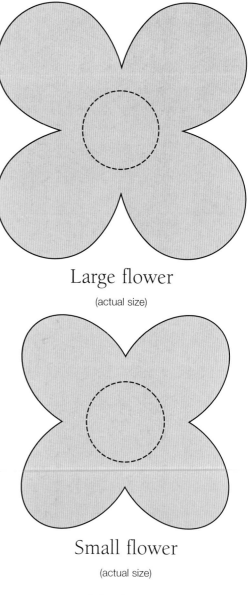

Large flower
(actual size)

Small flower
(actual size)

For Padded coat hanger

Page 130

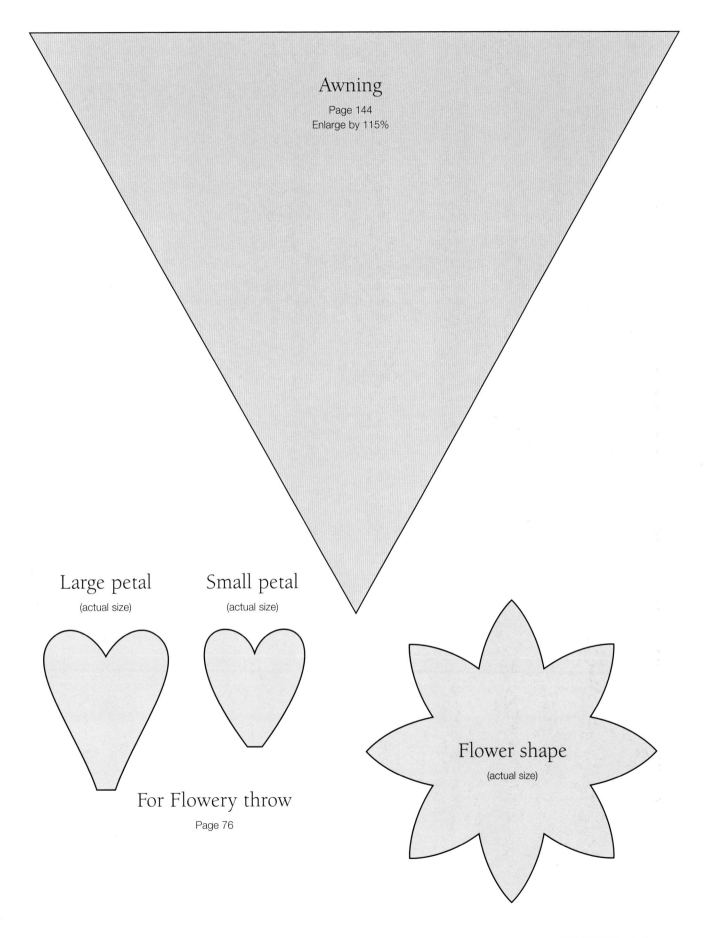

Awning

Page 144

Enlarge by 115%

Large petal

(actual size)

Small petal

(actual size)

For Flowery throw

Page 76

Flower shape

(actual size)

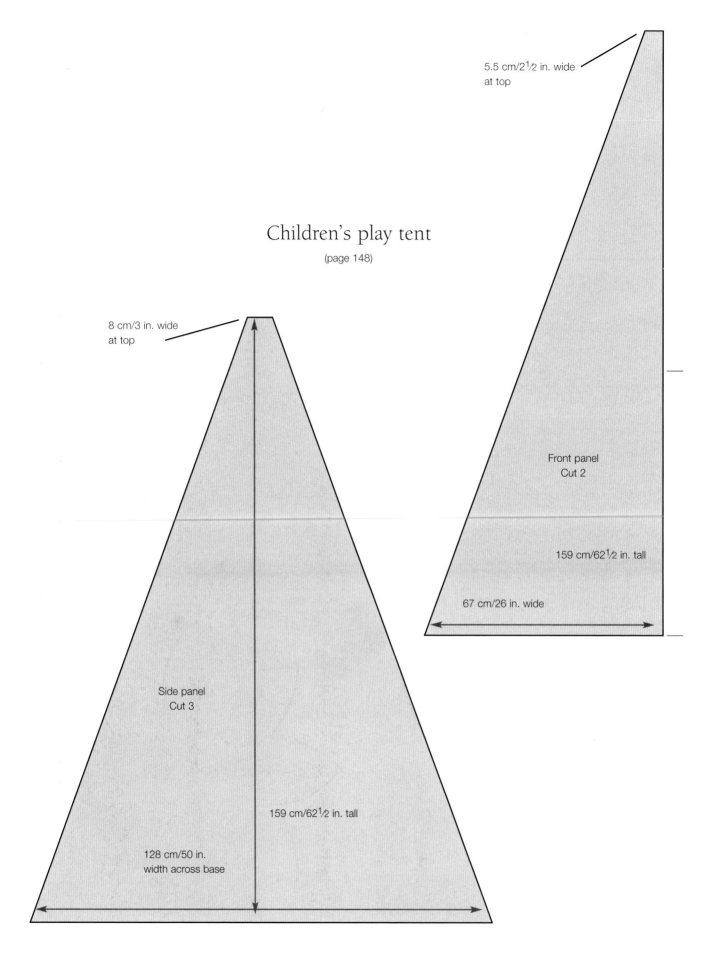

Children's play tent

(page 148)

5.5 cm/2½ in. wide at top

8 cm/3 in. wide at top

Front panel
Cut 2

159 cm/62½ in. tall

67 cm/26 in. wide

Side panel
Cut 3

159 cm/62½ in. tall

128 cm/50 in. width across base

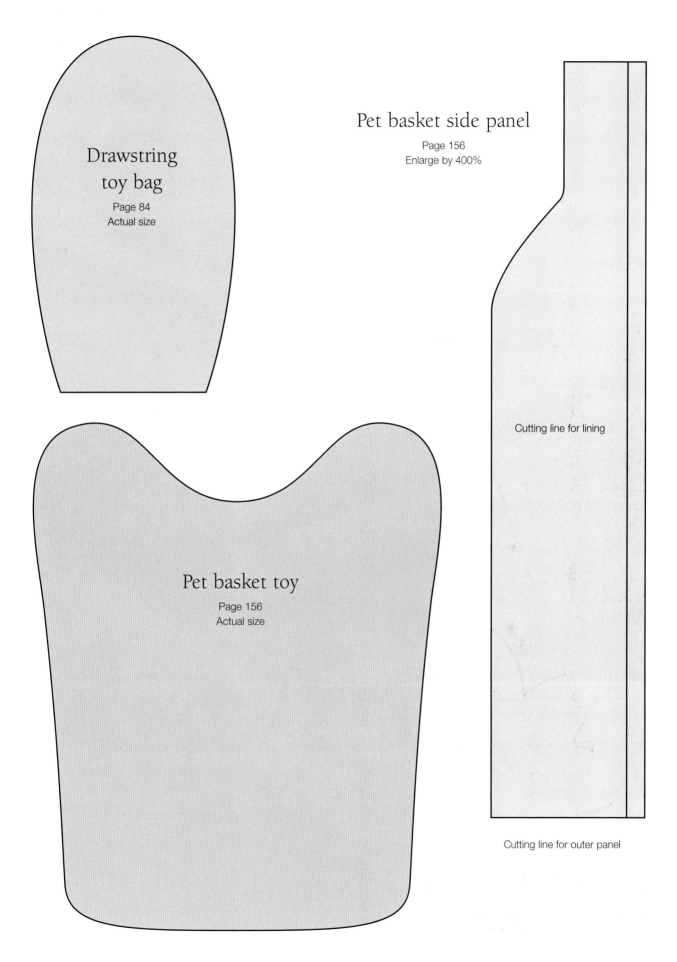

**Drawstring
toy bag**

Page 84
Actual size

Pet basket side panel

Page 156
Enlarge by 400%

Cutting line for lining

Cutting line for outer panel

Pet basket toy

Page 156
Actual size

Suppliers, index and acknowledgements

Suppliers

UK SUPPLIERS

The Button Queen
19 Marylebone Lane
London W1V 2NF
020 7935 1505
www.thebuttonqueen.co.uk

Laura Ashley
0871 230 2301
www.lauraashley.com

John Lewis
Oxford Street
London W1A 1EX
020 7629 7711
www.johnlewis.com

Liberty
Regent Street
London W1B 5AH
020 7734 1234
www.liberty.co.uk

The Quilt Room
20 West Street
Dorking
Surrey RH4 1BL
01306 740739
www.quiltroom.co.uk

Stitch In Time
293 Sandycombe Road
Kew
Surrey TW9 3LU
020 8948 8462
www.stitchintimeuk.com

Ian Mankin
109 Regents Park Road
Primrose Hill
London NW1 8UR
020 7722 0997
www.ianmankin.com

The Cloth House
47 Berwick Street
London W1F 8SJ
020 7437 5155
www.clothhouse.com

Cath Kidston
08450 262 440
www.cathkidston.co.uk

VV Rouleaux
102 Marylebone Lane
London W1U 2QD
020 7224 5179
www.vvrouleaux.com

US SUPPLIERS

Amy Butler
For stockists see
www.amybutlerdesign.com

Britex Fabrics
146 Geary Street
San Francisco
CA94108
415-392 2910
www.britexfabrics.com

Cia's Palette
4155 Grand Ave S.
Minneapolis
MN 55409
612-229 5227
www.ciaspalette.com

Purl Patchwork
147 Sullivan Street
New York
NY 10012
212-420 8798
www.purlsoho.com

Reprodepot Fabrics
413-527 4047
www.reprodepotfabrics.com

Tinsel Trading Company
47 West 38th Street
New York
NY 10018
212-730 1030
www.tinseltrading.com

Z and S Fabrics
681 S. Muddy Creek Road
Denver
PA 17157
717-336 4026
www.zandsfabrics.com

Index

Acknowledgements

I would like to thank everyone who worked on this book, especially Debbie Patterson for the beautiful photography and for making the shoots a lot of fun, Sarah Hoggett for editing the book with such calm and patience, Michael Hill for the lovely illustrations and David Fordham for the great design. At CICO, I would like to thank Sally Powell for all her assistance and support, and Cindy Richards for giving me the opportunity to do the book. You have all helped to make it a really enjoyable project.

Thank you to Maria Dahl for the loan of some lovely props. And thank you, thank you, thank you to Laurie for sharing our home with piles and piles of fabric, ribbons and buttons and still being enthusiastic about the whole project. A huge thank you to Gracie and Betty, my gorgeous girls, for giving me so many great ideas and lots of inspiration and for getting as excited about fabrics, haberdashery and making things as I do. You are stars!